VISIONS OF PARADISE

VISIONS OF *Paradise*

Images of Eden in the Cinema

WHEELER WINSTON DIXON

RUTGERS UNIVERSITY PRESS
NEW BRUNSWICK, NEW JERSEY, AND LONDON

Library of Congress Cataloging-in-Publication Data

Dixon, Wheeler W., 1950 –
Visions of paradise : images of Eden in the cinema / Wheeler Winston Dixon.
p. cm.
Includes bibliographical references and index.
ISBN-13: 978–0–8135–3797–9 (hardcover : alk. paper)
ISBN-13: 978–0–8135–3798–6 (pbk. : alk. paper)
1. Paradise in motion pictures. I. Title.
PN1995.9.P25D59 2006
791.43'672—dc22

2005020077

A British Cataloging-in-Publication record for this book is available from the British Library.

Book design by Adam B. Bohannon

Manufactured in the United States of America

FOR *Gwendolyn*

CONTENTS

ACKNOWLEDGMENTS

I wish to thank Leslie Mitchner of Rutgers University Press for her assistance in the preparation of this volume, as well as Maureen Moynihan for her diligent research work on this project. Dana Miller did her usual excellent work in typing the manuscript; Carol Inskip compiled the final index; Gwendolyn Audrey Foster offered fresh insights throughout the long writing of the text; and Virginia Clark and Shelle Sumners provided a superb job of copyediting the final manuscript. Brief portions of chapter 3 originally appeared in the journal *Film Criticism;* my thanks to Lloyd Michaels, editor, for permission to reprint this material here, in significantly revised form. Thanks also to Ron and Howard Mandelbaum of Photofest for the frame enlargement from *Portrait of Jennie* (1948), which serves as the cover image for this volume; the Jerry Ohlinger Archives and Robert Heller of Anthology Film Archives provided the stills that grace the text. Joy Ritchie, chair of the Department of English, and Richard Hoffmann, dean of the College of Arts and Sciences at the University of Nebraska, Lincoln, have consistently supported my work, which I deeply appreciate. I also wish to thank the various anonymous readers who helped me to clarify and shape this volume into its present form. Finally, I wish to salute the example of the many artists whose works are considered in this volume, in their unstinting desire to transcend the cares of everyday existence to create something ineffable, lasting, and beyond the scope of ordinary human experience; in short, an ecstatic experience that can be shared by all. To all these people, and to my many supportive colleagues, I offer my sincere thanks.

VISIONS OF PARADISE

[The] word "paradise" comes from the Old Persian *pairidaeza*, which originally meant a circular walled enclosure and came to be applied to royal parks. The Persian went into Hebrew as *pardes*, meaning, again, a park or garden. (It is used in this sense only three times in the Old Testament, of which the most important is the famous verse from the Song of Solomon: "A garden enclosed is my sister, my spouse; a garden locked, a fountain sealed.") In Greek, the word became *paradeisos* and kept its reference to parks and gardens. It was first used by Xenophon to describe the park, or *vivarium*, where King Cyrus kept the animals he hunted. At this stage, "paradise" did not mean an abstract state imagined in terms of angels and metaphysical ecstasy. Paradise was a place; it had concrete attributes, pleasures, inhabitants. . . .

—Robert Hughes, *Heaven and Hell in Western Art*

CHAPTER ONE

The Great Escape

Our world is dominated by images of escape. The pace of modern life is well-nigh insupportable, as we are assaulted from all sides by cell phone calls, telephone solicitations, and advertisements everywhere: television commercials (twenty minutes out of every prime-time hour is now the norm), pop-up ads on the Web, ads in taxis, on buses, on the sides of buildings, in newspapers, magazines, junk mail, and of course, the ubiquitous e-mail spam. We dream of ways of avoiding all this, of leaving the daily onslaught behind, of finding respite in a simulacrum of paradise. Travel magazines promise us carefree escapes on cruise ships, with abundant food, dancing, gambling, and stops in exotic ports of call; for the more adventurous, there are trips to remote parts of the world (usually the tropics) that offer excitement, the lure of the Other, and surcease from the conflicts of daily existence. And certainly the Web excels at presenting tempting opportunities for escape; indeed, making the most of this venue, the British conceptual artist Janice Kerbel, "dreaming of a holiday she could never afford, . . . designed an elaborate and convincing Website [www.bird-island.com] advertising real estate on a perfect, fictitious, uninhabited island [in the Caribbean] . . . [with] texts and drawings" (Higgie)—a balm to anyone bored, overworked, and in search of something beyond the realm of their daily lives.

As Kerbel notes in a recent exhibition of her work, her artworks "often have to do with making daydreams concrete . . . [relying] on a stock of secrets, lies, repetitions and codes that are meant to be unraveled and to lead to belief and trust" (De Appel Press Release). One could say much the same thing of contemporary advertising strategies that seek to lull us into believing that escape from the grind of quotidian existence is possible, and nowhere is this more apparent than in the cinema, which deals primarily in fantasy and escapism, and seeks to transport its audience members into an alternative universe for a few hours, all the better to return to one's normal existence. But occasionally a lucky few who have the financial backing and the desire to do so are actually able to slip the bonds of society, pull up stakes, and reinvent themselves in a seemingly idyllic and Edenic landscape. Motion-picture producer John Pierson was one such person who saw the chance to take a break from his hectic schedule of nonstop activity, although in the end he found his dream of paradise as evanescent as the images used to sell us "the dream of the tropics" in the cinema; no matter how much we may wish to invent a "perfect" world, reality persists in intruding.

In 1999 Pierson, the leading force behind Grainy Pictures, one of the most prominent and prolific producers of U.S.-based independent films, was experiencing, in his own words, a "spiritual crisis" (Heyman). After twenty-five years of securing funding for such breakthrough directors as Spike Lee, Kevin Smith, Matt Stone, and many other non-mainstream luminaries, Pierson was burned out by the business. Suddenly, an opportunity for escape presented itself. In February 2000, during the filming of the Independent Film Channel's series *Split Screen*, which Pierson produced, he learned of the existence of the 180 Meridian Cinema, a medium-sized movie house located on the remote island of Taveuni, Fiji, with 288 seats, an enthusiastic local audience (the island's population is roughly ten thousand people), and the added attraction of being some eight thousand miles from his Garrison, New York, home, far from the travails of the Manhattan independent film scene. Discovering that the Meridian's current owner intended to shutter the aging facility, Pierson impulsively decided to move his family to Taveuni and take over the theater, for an extended "working vacation" in paradise.

On August 3, 2002, Pierson and his wife and business partner, Janet, along with daughter Georgia, then fifteen, and son Wyatt, then twelve, journeyed to Taveuni to run the Meridian. They moved into "an old, wooden plantation house" (John Pierson, "Facts & Fibs") on the island, backed by the financial sponsorship of directors Lee, Smith, and Stone, who agreed that Pierson and his family needed a break from the pressures of the film business. The 180 Meridian Cinema, so-named because of its location near the International Date Line, had been in existence since the 1950s but had lately fallen on hard times. With the help of the local citizens the Piersons began to run a series of free nighttime film screenings, to the unbridled delight of the populace. Noted Pierson in an interview with Dave Kehr, after their return from their extended sojourn in the islands, "The old action heroes haven't died in Fiji. Stallone is still huge, Steven Seagal is still huge, and they love Chuck Norris" (Kehr B6). But as Kehr noted,

> the highlight in this experiment in bringing American movies to the edge of the world was seeing the *Three Stooges.* The theater, founded in the 1950s by an Indian entrepreneur, had its own print of [director Del Lord's] 1941 short *Some More of Samoa,* in which the Stooges visit a back lot South Pacific. Despite the film's politically incorrect depiction of island culture—the natives pop Curly into a big pot and try to boil him for dinner—Taveuni Islanders have been enjoying it literally for generations. The wild delight . . . began with the appearance of the Columbia logo. (Kehr B6)

Not that all was tranquil in Taveuni. A local group of Catholic priests objected to Pierson's screenings on the grounds that free admission to the films "encouraged a backsliding, handout mentality" and that the theater was fostering a "supernatural and cult-like" following

(John Pierson, "Showing Free Movies in Fiji"). With the help of the district officer, Pierson was able to fend off the priests' interference; despite the clerics' claim that there was "widespread distaste and dissatisfaction" with the free screenings ("Showing Free Movies in Fiji"), it was clear that the majority of the Taveuni Islanders were fully supportive of Pierson's venture. Nature, also, would have its say: in January 2003, Cyclone Ami pummeled the island and inflicted an enormous amount of damage, sparing little else other than the Pierson's villa and the 180 Meridian Cinema (John Pierson, "Facts & Fibs").

Although the Piersons had been assured that their living quarters were entirely safe, in March 2003 their home was burglarized, and though the loss was minimal, as Janet Pierson noted in her journal, "this was our fall from paradise. It wasn't the stuff per se . . . but it was the violation of trust. Which of our smiling, happy neighbors were the culprits? . . . It ended our ability to enjoy the purest of Fijian pleasures—the smiles of strangers" ("General Fiji Report—March"). A bicycle that the Pierson's son, Wyatt, owned was borrowed by a local boy who seemed reluctant to return it, or as Janet Pierson delicately put it, who was "struggling between his love of the bike and his friendship [with Wyatt]" ("General Fiji Report—March"). And perhaps most surprisingly, it seems that despite their passionate love affair with the cinema, the citizens of Taveuni don't really care how a given film ends. As John Pierson wrote in his own journal, "With each film I've played this year, 15% to 20% of the audience walks out in the last two minutes. Whether they've loved the picture, or merely found it tolerable, no matter how predictable it's been all along, they just don't feel a need to see how it ends" ("Isle of Forgotten Fans").

In short, despite the idyllic conditions (for the most part) and relaxed lifestyle, paradise wasn't all that it was cracked up to be. Although Georgia, the Piersons' daughter, had written in her diary that "What started out as a family joke has now become an unbelievable reality. . . . Instead of television, I have culture. Instead of boring, I have adventure. Instead of ordinary, I have paradise" ("Fiji Essay"), when the Piersons returned to the United States almost two years later, they did so with a genuine sense of regret, but also with something akin to relief that they could, if they wished, return to the more "wired" world.

Oddly, when Pierson originally asked for funding for this Quixotic venture from his friends and business associates, only Michael Moore refused to offer financial assistance, commenting simply, "Ugh, tell me this isn't happening" ("Isle of Forgotten Fans"). Perhaps Moore knew that the Piersons' quest was an impossible, maybe even colonialist dream. By the time the Piersons returned to the United States, it was clear that the entire affair had been a grand adventure, but far from the paradise lost that it might have initially seemed to be. What John and Janet Pierson were searching for was some momentary respite from the unceasing informational din of contemporary life, and they found it, but with its own price tag attached. Pierson had wanted to escape the tyranny of images that was ruling his existence and experience the cinema anew. He achieved his aim, but found that even in "paradise," there are compromises, drawbacks, and social negotiations that must be performed on a daily basis. In short, life continues, but at a different speed and with a different set of priorities and problems.

As the twenty-first century begins to unfold, we are left with a legacy of images from the twentieth century that is richer and more varied than that of any era before it. The innate technology of the cinema is that of the repetition of the image, with slight variations, assuring that literally billions of separate images have been recorded of the history of humankind in the twentieth century. War, famine, collapse, disaster, and scenes of violence and destruction abound in this record, if only because of the oft-quoted newspaper dictum, "If it bleeds, it leads." Whether recording fiction or reality, the motion picture camera has served as a mirror of our society for the past one hundred years, and with the dawn of digital technology, it is apparent that the cinema belongs to the technology of the past. Yet in this vast record of the past century there are also scenes of repose, rest, and sublime bliss, although they are too often obscured by the pornography of violence. For a brief moment these films offer us a vision of paradise, either earthly or heavenly, giving us some measure of solace from the demands of daily existence.

The Edenic cinema offers us glimpses of life free from strife, rich and meaningful, devoid of pain and privation. Indeed, these films offer the viewer a moment out of time, in which audience and cast members alike can partake of a vision of personal freedom and safety, a zone of privilege and protection that transcends the demands of daily existence. When we gaze upon these images of Eden in the dark, we see ourselves as we would like to be: surrounded by friends and family, free from harm, secure in a zone where time has no meaning and the rules of reality have been suspended. Many of these films come from the 1960s, perhaps the most "Edenic" decade in contemporary cinema, a period in which everything seemed possible and radical social change was taken for granted.

But even as these visions of paradise remain intangible, ephemeral, perpetually beyond our collective reach, they offer us a glimpse of what life might be like, of what our society can offer us, if we could only bridge the tantalizing gap between our needs and our desires. These films present a view of the world in which love, faith, and hope are all an integral part of the social landscape. As such, they offer a tonic to the darker visions of the twentieth century, in which the dreams of one generation collapsed into the realities of adulthood in the worlds of film noir, crime thrillers, war films, and films of betrayal and deceit. In this volume, then, I celebrate those films that present the world as we might wish it to be, if only we had the luxury of time, youth, and a sense of wonder.

And perhaps we don't. As Frank Schirrmacher notes, in the early part of the twenty-first century "we are having an encounter with reality. . . . we'll remember the time between 1950 and 2000 as a kind of paradise" (qtd. in Landler, 1, 3). Perhaps the sense of egalitarian Utopianism expressed in these pages is a uniquely twentieth-century phenomenon, when one considers the rapid cultural, political, and social shifts of the last five years. We began this century with our worst fears focused on the supposed Y2K (year 2000) phenomenon, which would ostensibly cause computers worldwide to crash. Then came the tragedy of September 11, 2001; the Iraq War starting in 2003; the reelection of President George W. Bush in 2004; and a nation that was deeply polarized—the Divided States of America. Where AM radio used to offer the countercultural strains of the Beatles, Bob Dylan, the Rolling Stones, and other sixties avatars, the AM band now belongs almost exclusively to Rush Limbaugh, Sean Hannity, and other purveyors of right-wing, homophobic, and xenophobic hate speech. Ashlee Simpson, Paris Hilton, Pink, and other disposable pop stars have become the new arbiters of social discourse, while Dylan appears in Victoria's Secret television advertisements and the remaining Beatles and the Rolling Stones allow their songs to be licensed for a wide variety of commercial promotions.

The pendulum must eventually swing back, or so it would seem, but how far will it drift into the margins of extremity before some sense of egalitarianism is restored? Is the era we are examining here lost beyond authentic recall? Was there ever a period when Eden truly was in our grasp? There must be a way back home, a way to find some common ground. This volume argues that Eden is attainable, even if the only proof that remains is the fact that we once seemed to have it within our collective grasp, only to see it vanish in a haze of merchandising, cross-promotions, and consumer exploitation. Yet the best is still within us, waiting to be brought out. If contemporary circumstances seem to militate against an Edenic revival, then perhaps our best lessons are to be learned from the past.

The Edenic cinema offers us an escape from the real world, which is replete with betrayal, illness, cupidity, and misfortune. In the midst of this imperfect zone of action, however, we must strive to create the best possible life for ourselves. No one ever said it would be perfect. No one ever said that it would last. But in the cinema such moments can be frozen forever, to be replayed at will, as long as there is a digital or analog copy of the work in question to restore us to Eden. When we go to the cinema, we, too, transcend our surroundings and are presented with a glimpse of the world as we might have it, outside the realm of actual human experience.

Lew Landers's *The Enchanted Forest* (1945) effectively embraces this theme of an Edenic return to nature in its tale of Old John (Harry Davenport), a reclusive hermit who lives in California's Redwood Forest. Old John has lived in the forest so long that it has become his home, and he communes with the animals as equal beings, rather than as pets or beasts of burden. When loggers try to move in on his domain, Old John fights back with the help of his animal friends, sabotaging the loggers' efforts. One day, in the aftermath of a train crash at the edge of the forest, Old John finds an infant boy and raises him as his own. Jackie (William Severn) soon learns the ways of the forest and is eventually reunited with his mother, while Old John manages, with the help of Steven Blaine (Edmund Lowe) and Anne (Brenda Joyce), to protect his pastoral way of life forever and save the forest from commercial predation.

This oddly prophetic film, produced by the mini-studio Producers Releasing Corporation and shot in Cinecolor, the poor man's Technicolor, struck a responsive chord with end-of-the-war audiences who were tired of endless newsreels of disaster and hyperpatriotic war films and musicals. What is most striking about *The Enchanted Forest* is its strong ecological message; the forest is a resource that needs to be protected and preserved, not endlessly exploited for personal or financial gain. In a cinematic landscape populated by a seemingly unceasing parade of wars, disasters, horrific monsters, and hard-boiled criminals, *The Enchanted Forest* is a unique exemplar in 1940s cinema, almost without precedent. *The Enchanted Forest* posits that humankind can only be satisfied when it places nature on a level of importance equal with human striving for intellectual or economic accomplishment.

1. Harry Davenport in Lew Landers's *The Enchanted Forest* (1945). Photograph courtesy of The Jerry Ohlinger Archives.

John Cromwell's *The Enchanted Cottage* (1945), another post–World War II film, tackles a similar theme but relates it to human affliction, rather than the preservation of the wild. Oliver Bradford (Robert Young) and Laura Pennington (Dorothy McGuire) are two marginalized people somewhat like Harry Davenport's Old John in *The Enchanted Forest*, who exists in a state of blissful self-exile. For Oliver and Laura, however, the separation has been enforced by society, and not personal preference. Wounded in the war, Oliver is a battle-scarred ex-GI whose face has been disfigured, while Laura lacks the external attributes of conventional "beauty" and cannot find a partner for marriage. As the film's tagline suggests, "the whole town whispered about these two," especially when they become romantically attached during a stay at a cottage where Laura works and Oliver was to spend his honeymoon before his war injuries. Oliver's original fiancée, Beatrice Alexander (played by the ever-glacial Hillary Brooke), wants nothing to do with Oliver after his disfigurement. For her part, when Laura attends a local USO dance, no one will dance with her because of her "plain" appearance, driving her deeper into despair.

But the cottage has a secret, revealing the inner beauty of its inhabitants through the mediating agency of Major John Hillgrove (Herbert Marshall), a blind composer who serves as the film's narrator. When Laura and Oliver marry, it is simply a way to avoid a world that has rejected them and avoid further psychic damage. But as their love blossoms, their exterior aspect begins to reflect their interior love for each other and they become conventionally attractive, but only to each other. A surprise visit from Oliver's family proves that the exterior "beauty" they see is for their eyes only—to the world outside, they are still a scarred man and a "homely" woman.

Yet even as this realization sinks in, Oliver and Laura realize that they have found a genuine love for each other, and it is *this* that makes them beautiful to each other. With its message of tolerance, inner beauty, and compassion, even when everyday society refuses to recognize their social values, *The Enchanted Cottage* is a peculiarly Edenic tale, suggesting that when one departs from the Garden, the world will judge a person's worth through exterior factors alone, as is often the case. As Gilles Deleuze has noted, "The screen itself is the cerebral membrane where immediate and direct confrontations take place between the past and the future, the inside and the outside, at a distance impossible to determine, independent of any fixed point" (qtd. in Martin 83). For Oliver and Laura, the membrane of their individuated consciousness resides solely within the confines of *The Enchanted Cottage*; when they attempt a reentry into the actual world, they are rebuffed as outsiders. It is significant, as well, that Major Hillgrove, the film's narrator, is blind, and relies upon his music as a tool to relate to the outside world, a world he cannot apprehend through visual means.

William Dieterle's *Portrait of Jennie* (1948) provides another "moment out of time" for its two protagonists, Eben Adams (Joseph Cotten) and the ethereal Jennie Appleton (Jennifer Jones), who also create their own world. Eben is a New York City artist who has no faith in his work; though he continually applies himself to his craft, he is unable to make it come to life, or to sell enough of his work to keep body and soul together. But in *Portrait of Jennie,* postwar New York is a cozy, peaceful place, and Eben is able to get meals on the cuff at a local Italian restaurant, while he strolls through a bucolic Central Park during the day, searching for inspiration. One morning Eben meets Jennie, a talkative young girl who refers to the past as if it were the present, and

2. Eben Adams (Joseph Cotten) and the ethereal Jennie Appleton (Jennifer Jones) in William Dieterle's *Portrait of Jennie* (1948). Photograph courtesy of The Jerry Ohlinger Archives.

seems to exist in a world of her own. Whenever he seems to be getting close to some real communication with Jennie, Eben finds that she has mysteriously vanished.

Returning to the park in search of Jennie over the next few months, Eben finds her older, and changed; he is almost irresistibly drawn to her image. Inspired, Eben paints Jennie's portrait and finds that it represents an artistic and financial breakthrough for him; he has finally found his ideal subject. At length, however, Eben discovers that Jennie is the ghost of a woman who died years ago in a violent storm. Compelled by his attraction to Jennie, Eben travels to the location of her death, where the storm appears anew and washes Jennie out to sea forever. In her final moments with Eben, Jennie tells him that their love will transcend time and become immortal. The still on the frontispiece of this book, taken directly from the film as a frame enlargement, suggests at once the fanciful and Edenic atmosphere in which *Portrait of Jennie* exists; here Manhattan, far from being the big city, is the domain of star-crossed lovers, who depend upon the kindness of tolerant restaurateurs and art patrons who seemingly exist only to keep the lovers' dream alive.

In *Portrait of Jennie*, the world is a place of attainable triumph, in which dreams do come true, in which the unreal can attain substance and actuality through faith. Jennie is only as real as Eben's imagination, and the vicissitudes of metropolitan life do not really exist for the two lovers. The city, rather, exists as a backdrop for them, suggesting a connection between the paradisiacal and the actual, as if Heaven, or its cinematic simulacrum, is a tangible presence in the world of human affairs. Eben's dream of becoming a painter is realized only when he makes contact with, and is guided by, a vision that exists outside of time, and certainly outside of the borough of Manhattan. The world that Eben and Jennie exist in is simultaneously real and imaginary; it is the world as we would wish to have it, the world of the everyday made magical.

The world created by Dieterle in *Portrait of Jennie* is perhaps the ultimate late-1940s studio construct, composed of matte paintings, rear projection, cyclorama backdrops, and studio special effects, in which the living inhabit the cinematic world created for them almost as an afterthought. Although there are some genuine exterior shots in the film, for the most part *Jennie* exists only so long as the camera is running and the key lights for the film stay correctly in place. It is, in a word, synthetic; a zone inhabited only by figures in the narrative, but existing for them alone, and having no physical reality other than that which we see on the screen. As the 1940s gave way to the 1950s and 1960s, films became more naturalistic, and often were shot on location, as if to acknowledge their link to the world we live in. But with the end of the twentieth century, synthetic spectacle once again came back into fashion with such films as James Cameron's *Titanic* (1997), the *Star Wars* series, and the rise in popularity of video games. Even as the Internet and the Web put us more "in touch," they also separate us from one another and create "limit zones" of communication.

There is no real human contact in the world of video games or computer-generated imagery (CGI); all is illusory, nontactile, divorced from the physical world. There is a reassuring aspect to this, inasmuch as it exists entirely within the zone of fantasy and allows us to escape from the mundane problems of existence. The rise of video art, from its beginnings with such artists as Nam June Paik, Charlotte Moorman, and Bill Viola, has signaled the embrace of an entirely new terrain, in which that which is real is transmuted into something altogether different; a place that we can visit only for the duration of the work we are viewing. It is real, but unattainable; we can virtually "visit" this new world, but we can never live there. It is composed of pixels, light, ones, and zeros, and would seem to be as far removed as possible from the hyperstylized world of the classical Hollywood cinema. And yet many contemporary video artists hearken back to the values of the Hollywood studio film, in their embrace of the artificial to create an alternative universe. Indeed, even as the technology of the moving image becomes more advanced, it seems that many aspects of the creation of that image remain deeply rooted in the tradition of costume drama, or pantomime.

For the Japanese visual artist Mariko Mori, the Edenic world is an interior landscape exteriorized through the use of costumes, props, elaborate sets, and 3-D video installations. Born in Tokyo in 1967, Mori attended "a traditional, highly structured girls' high school . . . which required uniforms with prescribed skirt length and fixed hairstyles" (Eliel 27). After graduation Mori worked part-time as a fashion model while studying fashion design, but soon realized that "a model is actually just a doll that changes clothes. Modeling [did] not enable me to express myself" (qtd. in Eliel 27). To correct this, Mori began to stage a series of elaborate tableaux, serving as "producer, director, set and costume designer and star" in her own synthetic environments, to re-create not only her own persona but also the world she was forced to inhabit (Eliel 27). In such early works as *Warrior* (1994), Mori re-created herself as a "stereotypical superhero[ine] and the eponymous Japanese warrior" (Eliel 28).

These early attempts at reinvention were followed by a series of increasingly elaborate visual constructs, including *Miko no Inori* (1996), convincingly depicting Mori as a vacant-eyed ice princess; *Play with Me* (1994), in which Mori poses as a mechanized sex toy in front of a Tokyo video game arcade; *Subway* (1994), demonstrating the ability of Mori's futuristic costume to displace her from the mundane normality of a typical scene on the Tokyo underground; *Tea Ceremony III* (1995), displaying Mori in streamlined flight attendant's garb, serving tea to passing Japanese businessmen; and her early signature image, *Birth of a Star* (1995), in which Mori appears as the ultimate throwaway pop star, existing in a brightly colored, deeply superficial world of multicolored plastic spheres floating in space, plugged into a set of headphones blasting the latest ultradisposable pop music.

In the appropriately titled *Empty Dream* (1995), Mori documented a synthetic indoor "beach" installation in downtown Tokyo, where citizens frolic on a ready-made beach under an ersatz sun, swimming in a saltwater pool with an artificial horizon that suggests the infinity of the earth's horizon. By *Nirvana* (1996–1997), however, Mori was turning inward, rather than documenting the intrinsic superficiality of her corporeal existence. *Nirvana* is still deeply indebted to the star system that Mori so deeply embraces, as she positions herself as a sort of deity at the center of a 3-D video universe, existing outside of space and time, worshipped by a group of pixies who float through the video frame to create a ring around her central imagistic presence, reminding the viewer of nothing so much as electronically manufactured angels, refugees from an alternative electronic universe. As she is adored by her genderless acolytes, Mori drifts through the frame in traditional Japanese religious costumes, singing and making Buddhist hand gestures, *mudras,* which suggest both distance and detached compassion.

In contrast to Mori's other constructed alternative worlds, her presence in *Nirvana* is mediated by the digital manipulation of her body through CGI technology and the cerebral tension created by the eyestrain inherent in the polarized 3-D process Mori employs in the work. Mori in *Nirvana* is a moving, if not precisely "living" presence; the artificiality of her sacred presence is underscored by the cartoon-like design of the computer-game "angels" who witness her presence. Yet, as the brief video, lasting only a few minutes, unspools before the viewer, one gets the sense of having been transported to an alternate universe, complete with its own immutable logic and devoid of pain, suffering, or loss. The world of *Nirvana* is, if artificial, *complete;* it encompasses Mori's vision of herself as a being removed from both the audience and from the world that she creates as well as inhabits. Still later installations, such as *Burning Desire* (1996–1998), continue this Buddhist preoccupation with self-contemplation and the transcendence of the real to attain a state of noncorporeality. In *Burning Desire,* Mori's floating, scathed figure is encircled by a multicolored rainbow, while four other images of the artist are seated on a barren mud landscape, seemingly consumed by sacred flames that illuminate but do not burn. Mori's vision is thus transformative not only for her own presence within the work, but also for her audience and in her use of the photographic and video medium to present herself to the world as a supernatural, semi-angelic harbinger of the new era of interconnectedness, in which celebrity is mediated by televisual exposure, printed ads, and momentary public approbation.

While Mori represents the new wave of visual experimentation in search of paradise, the late Stan Brakhage, one of the most prolific experimental filmmakers the medium has yet produced, created in his lifetime no less than 370 films, most of which sought to re-see the world through a child's eye and re-vision the existing universe as an entirely uncharted field of personal inquiry. Beginning with the elegiac and adolescent *Interim* in 1952, and the drunken escapism of the landmark *Desistfilm* (1954), in which a group of teenagers hold an impromptu party in a deserted shack, scatter into the woods, and then return to confront one couple who have stayed behind to make love, Brakhage charted an alternative visual lexicon in which innocence was the paramount characteristic, with the human body and the earth one congruent sphere of consciousness. Throughout the 1950s, as a life-giving tonic to the shameful conduct of the House Un-American Activities Committee and such alarmist propaganda films as Leo McCarey's *My Son John* (1952), Brakhage documented the activities of his family at their house in Rollinsville, Colorado, where the personal became emblematic for the desires of an entire generation of cineastes. For the most part, Brakhage's films are silent, to concentrate on the veracity of the image to the exclusion of any competing levels of discourse. In *Centuries of June* (1955, made with the collage artist Joseph Cornell), Brakhage documented the lazy eternity of a small-town summer. In *Loving* (1956), Brakhage sought to capture "the act of lovemaking on film without shame or prurience, depicting the greens of the forest, the flesh tones of the lovers, the browns of earth, the sky and the sun [. . . evolving into . . .] an expression of loving in which the light consumes everything except the flesh of loving" (qtd. in *Film-*

Makers' Cooperative Catalogue No. 4, 20; hereafter referred to as FMC). In *Window Water Baby Moving* (1959), a film that documented the birth of his daughter, Brakhage created a document that critic Archer Winsten described as "so forthright, so full of primitive wonder and love, so far beyond civilization in its acceptance that it becomes an experience like few in the history of the movies" (qtd. in FMC 20).

Wedlock House: An Intercourse (1959) documented the first months of Brakhage's marriage to his wife Jane, but although the film was praised for its unrelenting honesty when first released, and Jane Brakhage was certainly a willing coproducer in the film's construction, toward the end of Brakhage's life he acknowledged that, in retrospect, *Wedlock House* and his other "family" films cut too close to the bone for Jane, in a way that made her feel uncomfortable. In an interview with Suranjan Ganguly, Brakhage admitted that

> when an artist mixes his working process with his daily life then there is a psychological imposition on other people who are involved. . . . It was more pervasive and in that sense more invasive of activities within the home which I now feel should be an area of privacy. There was an enormous invasion also of Jane's and my privacy as well. So while I certainly achieved a better relationship vis-à-vis the children in the act of making those films than what I had inherited, it didn't go as far as I had hoped—all of which goes to show why [my] 29-year-old marriage . . . a constant point of reference within my art-making, finally collapsed. . . . I think [Jane] felt used by the process coming through and directed by me, so I took her word for it then and still do now and feel condemned that a part of me couldn't see as well into her condition as it could with regard to the children. It must have been a terrible imposition on her. (Ganguly 143)

Thus, even in Eden, the tensions of human existence are always an omnipresent factor. As Brakhage persisted in his documentation project in such films as *Thigh Line Lyre Triangular* (1961), he was also conscious of the encroachment of the outside world, most notably expressed by the presence of a television in the Brakhages' mountain home, which more often than not brought bad news rather than good. In *Oh Life—A Woe Story—The A Test News* (1963), Brakhage shot images directly off the television screen, directly confronting the cornucopia of hate, fear, ignorance, consumerism, and death-worship that was being televisually funneled into his otherwise idyllic home. In *Mothlight* (1963), Brakhage did away with the camera entirely, creating the film out of moth wings taped directly onto the film between two strips of clear Mylar tape; the resultant film almost didn't make it through the printer at the laboratory, but the final image is worth the intense effort, as a series of moths seem to return to life through the medium of cinematic reanimation, long after their collective demise.

By the early 1960s, Brakhage was consumed with the production of his epic film *Dog Star Man* (1961–1964), recently selected by the Library of Congress for inclusion in the National Film Registry (Ganguly 139). At the same time he began a series of 8mm *Songs* (the bulk of Brakhage's work was shot in 16mm), in which he attempted to make even more personal statements about his life, family, and work. The *Songs* series eventually gave birth to more than twenty films of varying lengths, including the epic *Song XXIII: 23rd Psalm Branch, Part 1* (1966), another attempt to come to terms with the ceaseless death imagery of commercial television. As Brakhage commented in an interview in the *Los Angeles Free Press* at the time of the film's first public screenings,

> we had moved around a lot and we had settled down enough a year and a half ago. . . . So we got a TV. And that was something in the house that I could simply not photograph, simply could not deal with visually. It was pouring forth war guilt, primarily, into the household in a way that I wanted to relate to, if I was guilty, but I had feelings . . . of the qualities of guilt and I wanted to have it real for me and I wanted to deal with it. And, I mean, it was happening on all the programs—on the ads as well as drama and even the comedies, and of course the news programs.

> And I had to deal with that. It finally became such a crisis that I knew I couldn't deal directly with TV, but perhaps I could make or find out why war was all that unreal to me. . . . (qtd. in *FMC* 27)

Gradually, as the 1960s gave way to the sleeker, structuralist 1970s, and Brakhage had seemingly exhausted his family's patience and his own resilience as a filmmaker with the pursuit of an elusive Edenic lifestyle, the filmmaker turned to increasingly externalized projects such as *Eyes* (1970), which documents the daily life of a Pittsburgh policeman as he patrols the streets of his decaying city; *Deus Ex* (1971), a film depicting hospital work as a series of abstract crises; and most notoriously, *The Act of Seeing with One's Own Eyes* (1971), in which Brakhage directly confronts his and our mortality by entering the autopsy room of a morgue and recording in graphic (though, as always, completely silent) detail the evisceration of various corpses by physicians who have long ago become inured to the violent spectacle in which they are participants. Toward the end of his life, Brakhage became more and more interested in entirely abstract films, as if dealing with the life-essence of the filmic medium itself, painting directly on the film to create such late films as *Water for Maya* (2000), a tribute to the pioneering experimental filmmaker Maya Deren. Stan Brakhage was, in many senses, one of the first true "dropouts" in American society, along with the Beats and later the hippies, though he had no patience for the self-indulgence of the hippie movement and was repulsed by the drug culture that exploded in the 1960s.

Indeed, in the early 1960s Brakhage withdrew all his films from the Film-Makers' Cooperative in New York as a gesture of protest against the films of Andy Warhol, which were, at that time, also distributed by the Cooperative. Only after lengthy negotiations conducted by Jonas Mekas and others did Brakhage restore his films to public availability, and only after he had viewed a great number of Warhol's films at the Co-op offices and had become convinced, despite his earlier reservations, that Warhol was a genuine artist and not just a publicity-seeking exploitationist. A fiercely independent patriarch, Brakhage continued to make films up until his death in 2003, still searching for an Edenic existence that, in the end, eluded him, no matter how spirited his pursuit of domestic and familial paradise may have been. For Brakhage, the vision of Eden remained tantalizingly close yet constantly transient, confined to the medium of the cinema alone. In film he sought to transmute the vicissitudes of existence into a coherent and fluid system of psychic discourse, and succeeded, only to discover that the same discipline could not be brought to bear on his own life. Like all of us, Brakhage was mortal; in Eden, we are all eternal.

Brakhage worked outside the boundaries of traditional cinema practice, and yet, for a time, even this most uncompromising of artists worked for a commercial ad agency. Although "his films were rarely seen outside the experimental film community, there is one bit of film that Brakhage is supposed to have made that practically everyone in America has seen—the original shot of a Downy fabric softener bottle falling in slow motion into a plump pile of towels" ("Stan Brakhage Biography"). This image of the magical in the everyday represents a perfect melding of the domestic with the Edenic; a space in which even the most routine chores can become magical.

In the world of the commercial cinema, the search for the "perfect life" is equally intense, albeit more directly linked to concerns of narrative, audience expectations, and the reification of social and gender roles. Eden is above all a state of mind, not relegated to any one place or time. The lure of the tropics is the same as the lure of Manifest Destiny, the desire to escape beyond existing frontiers into newer ones. The most popular of film genres until the inception of the science-fiction boom in the early 1950s (when space became "the final frontier," as the opening narration of *Star Trek* would have it), the Western was a cinematic staple that crossed all boundaries of class, race, and gender.

Many Westerns, naturally, thrived on conflict—often of the most primitive and simplistic kind—but as with most myth cycles, the Western in one of its most classic forms existed as a simple paradigm: Eden found, Eden threatened, Eden reclaimed, often through violence. Yet many of the most popular Westerns of the late 1940s and 1950s seemed to dispense with any threats in the most obligatory and desultory manner; what the audiences came to see was space that was yet unspoiled, untamed, and open to seemingly endless exploration.

Westerns came in all budget ranges, from the highest to the lowest. Producers Releasing Corporation, for example, specialized in a series of Westerns shot in two or three days, mostly directed by Sam Newfield (also known as Sherman Scott and Peter Stewart to hide his absurdly prolific tracks), such as *Prairie Pals* (1942, as Peter Stewart), *Sheriff of Sage Valley* (1942, as Sherman Scott), *Tumbleweed Trail* (1942, as Peter Stewart), *Rolling Down the Great Divide* (1942, as Peter Stewart), *The Lone Rider in Cheyenne* (1942, as himself), and many others. Monogram Pictures, another Poverty Row company, also produced numerous Westerns on minimal budgets, as did Columbia, Universal, and the rest of the major studios. Beyond these bargain-basement productions, more ambitious Westerns were also produced, aimed at specific groups of filmgoers.

Fritz Lang's *The Return of Frank James* (1940) and *Western Union* (1941), both made for Twentieth Century Fox, are Technicolor elegies to the Old West and to the pioneer spirit that broke the plains. Lang, a German émigré most famous for such fatalistic films as *Metropolis* (1927) and M (1931), fled Germany in 1933 to avoid working for the Nazis and eventually landed in Hollywood, where he soon became much in demand for his ability to keep an eye on the budget and the film moving at a rapid clip. Signed as a contract director to Fox in the late 1930s, Lang shot *The Return of Frank James* as his first color film, although he referred to the project as "an assignment, but I was interested" (qtd. in

Bogdanovich 42). The success of that film temporarily typecast Lang, perhaps the least likely director to be associated with the Western, as an expert in the genre, and the lavishly budgeted *Western Union* was the result, also shot in Technicolor. Lang's view of the West is perhaps the most sentimental of any of the directors discussed here, a fact that is surprising in view of the bleakness of many of his most famous films. But for *Western Union*, Lang chose to depict the West as it was remembered, rather than as a historical reconstruction. As Lang told future director Peter Bogdanovich in 1965,

> after *Western Union* was released something happened that I liked very, very much—vain as every man is. I got a letter from a club of Old Timers in Flagstaff [Arizona] which said, "Dear Mr. Lang, we have seen *Western Union* and this picture describes the West much better than the best pictures that have been made about the West. . . ." [But] I don't think this picture depicted the West as it *was*; maybe it lived up to certain dreams, illusions—what the Old Timers *wanted* to remember of the old West. (qtd. in Bogdanovich 44)

Roy Rogers and Dale Evans appeared in a series of program musical Westerns for Republic, including William Witney's *Home in Oklahoma* (1946), Frank McDonald's *Rainbow Over Texas* (1946), and numerous other films that extolled the virtues of small-town life and the comparative personal and spatial freedom afforded by the Great Plains. In R. G. Springsteen's *Homesteaders of Paradise Valley* (1947), Allan Lane plays comic-book hero Red Ryder with Robert Blake as his young sidekick, Little Beaver, in a simplistic narrative of betrayal and redemption. Red wants homesteaders to move to Paradise Valley, and he strikes a deal with a group of local businessmen from Central City for half-interest in Paradise Valley in return for their building a dam to supply the valley with needed water for irrigation and livestock. When the dam is completed, the corrupt financiers seek to divert all the water to Central City (a neatly named locale that suggests all that is cosmopolitan and therefore suspect).

The film's narrative closure comes as no surprise; after a series of double crosses, Red Ryder restores the water rights to the new citizens of Paradise Valley, and their Edenic dream is secured. Springsteen, who directed Westerns for most of his career, was a competent genre craftsman who knew how to extract the most from each production dollar. In contrast to his numerous other Westerns, however, such as *Arizona Cowboy* (1950), *Toughest Man in Arizona* (1952), *He Rides Tall* (1964), and *Showdown* (1963), the world depicted in *Homesteaders of Paradise Valley*, though momentarily imperiled, is a zone of peace, plenty, and rugged natural beauty.

Other Western auteurs find in the West a place of violent beauty. Anthony Mann, who began his career directing noir films in the late 1940s, found a new locale for his energy and pictorial vitality in such classic Westerns as *Bend of the River* (1952), *The Last Frontier* (1955), *The Man from Laramie* (1955), *The Tin Star* (1957), and *Man of the West* (1958), to name just a few of his many works. Mann's Westerns are violent but clean, reveling in the freedom that the West represents, perhaps the last zone of individual action left for women and men. Budd Boetticher created his own cinematic canon in the "Ranown" series, starring Randolph Scott, which depicted the West as a zone of social discourse governed by a specific set of rules and regulations that one obeyed as an act of honor. In *Seven Men from Now* (1956), *The Tall T* (1957), *Comanche Station* (1960), *Buchanan Rides Alone* (1958), *Westbound* (1959), and *Ride Lonesome* (1959), Boetticher created a world "where the ambiguous drama of individualism can be played out . . . Boetticher's West is simply *the world*, a philosophical ground over which his pilgrims move to be confronted with existential choices" not of their own making (Kitses 93). Sam Peckinpah's brief career as an essayist of Western violence is nevertheless tinged with an obvious patina of regret and/or nostalgia for times past; in *The Deadly Companions* (1961), *Major Dundee* (1965), *The Wild Bunch* (1969), *The Ballad of Cable Hogue* (1970), and *Pat*

Garrett and Billy the Kid (1973), Peckinpah's brutal vision is mitigated by his sense that the old West has gone forever, and that only honor and personal responsibility can redeem man in the modern world (see Kitses for more on these gifted auteurs).

Above all, the Western is a place of personal renewal and natural beauty, where one can prove oneself in a potentially hostile landscape and find beauty in the most unlikely details. John Ford's *3 Godfathers* (1948) also took a rather Edenic view of the West, casting three itinerant cowboys in the role of surrogate parents when they find an infant abandoned on the trail. Indeed, Ford's elegiac view of the West centered on one specific location: Monument Valley, Arizona, where he returned time and time again to re-create his vision of the nation's past. In such films as *She Wore a Yellow Ribbon* (1949), *Rio Grande* (1950), *The Searchers* (1956), and *Two Rode Together* (1961), Ford's elegiac vision of Manifest Destiny echoed the romantic paintings of Frederic Remington, who brought to the American populace the first visualization of the West as a place of promise and hope.

In Ford's *The Man Who Shot Liberty Valance* (1962), Tom Doniphon (John Wayne) brings a cactus rose to his fiancée, Hallie (Vera Miles) —a flower sprouting out of a maze of thorns, yet a rose, nonetheless. And Ford, perhaps appropriately, has the last word about the pull of memory and nostalgia in the Western in the famous exchange between Ransom Stoddard (James Stewart) and newspaper editor Maxwell Scott (Carleton Young), when Stoddard at last clears up the mystery of who exactly *did* shoot the vicious outlaw Liberty Valance (Lee Marvin). Stoddard has built a political career on his supposed killing of Valance, but it was Doniphon, in fact, who shot Valance from a nearby alley during a gunfight, unnoticed by the rest of the townspeople. When Stoddard finishes confessing the truth to Scott, essentially telling him that his entire life has been built on a lie, Scott balls up the exposé he'd written and throws it into the fire. "You're not going to use the story, Mr. Scott?" Stoddard asks. Scott shakes his head, adding, "This is the West, sir. When the legend becomes fact, print the legend." For most of us, the West remains the location of legend, escape, and self-reliance; it is a new world where we may reinvent ourselves and begin our lives anew.

One of Ford's last films, *Donovan's Reef*, is of particular interest because it partakes not of the West, but rather of the lure of the tropics, as the key members of Ford's cinematic stock company (John Wayne, Lee Marvin, Dick Foran, Cesar Romero, Mike Mazurki, Edgar Buchanan, and many others) forsake the Great Plains for the fictitious South Sea island of Haleakoloha (the film was actually shot in Kauai, Hawaii), where two old navy friends, Michael "Guns" Donovan (John Wayne) and Aloysius "Boats" Gilhooley (Lee Marvin), celebrate their shared birthday each year by staging an epic fight in Michael's bar, Donovan's Reef. As many critics have noted, the film has a certain sense of timelessness about it, as if Wayne, Marvin, Romero, and the other key actors have already died and are now happily ensconced in Heaven,

3. John Wayne and Elizabeth Allen fall in love in a Hawaiian paradise in John Ford's *Donovan's Reef* (1963). Photograph courtesy of The Jerry Ohlinger Archives.

reenacting the rituals of their past. Indeed, this was Wayne's last film with Ford, and Ford used his own yacht, *The Araner*, as a floating command post during the film's shooting, suggesting that perhaps when the West ends, the realm of paradise begins.

If the Western has long served as a narrative location for Edenic discourse, stories situated on a tropical island paradise have also long captured our imagination, appealing to our desire to escape to a simpler, more beautiful world, as evidenced in Ford's adventure in the tropics in *Donovan's Reef*. This "island paradise" motif has been reflected in numerous films of the 1920s to the present and remains a potent trope even today. Robert Flaherty's *Moana* (1926), also known as *Moana: A Romance of the Golden Age*, documents a life of ease and tranquility among the Polynesian natives on a Samoan island, focusing on the adolescence of a young man, Moana. Much of the action in the film is staged, showing daily activities such as fishing, cooking, and other tasks. Flaherty depicts Samoan life as virtually Utopian, in sharp contrast to Flaherty's initial foray into "ethnographic" filmmaking, the equally transparently staged and manipulated *Nanook of the North* (1922).

In F. W. Murnau and Robert Flaherty's dark *Tabu* (1931), paradise remains intact only so long as civilization, and in particular commerce and alcohol, are not allowed to pollute the carefree life of the islands. The love story depicted in *Tabu* between a young woman, Reri (Anne Chevalier), and Matahi, a pearl diver (playing himself), is as troubled as the film's genesis. Begun as a collaboration between Flaherty and German expressionist F. W. Murnau (most famous for *Nosferatu*, his version of *Dracula*, made in 1922), the film was shot on location on the island of Bora Bora, and the two directors soon clashed over their differing approaches to the material. When Flaherty withdrew, Murnau was left to take over the film, and he transformed the film's narrative from a straightforward love story into a tale of doomed romance. *Tabu*

4. Ceremonial celebration in F. W. Murnau and Robert Flaherty's *Tabu* (1931). Photograph courtesy of The Jerry Ohlinger Archives.

was photographed when Bora Bora was still an unsullied location of natural beauty, and despite the patina of Murnau's dark narrative closure, the film remains a genuine artifact of unspoiled beauty. As Jonathan Rosenbaum comments,

> Filmed entirely in the South Seas in 1929 with a nonprofessional cast and gorgeous cinematography by Floyd Crosby, [*Tabu*] began as a collaboration with documentarist Robert Flaherty, who still shares credit for the story, though clearly the German romanticism of Murnau predominates, above all in the heroic poses of the islanders and the fateful diagonals in the compositions. The simple plot is an erotic love story involving a young woman who

> becomes sexually taboo when she is selected by an elder to replace a sacred maiden who has just died; an additional theme is the corrupting power of "civilization." The exquisite tragic ending—conceived musically and rhythmically as a gradually decelerating diminuendo—is one of the pinnacles of silent cinema.

Tabu is a curious hybrid, a film that is simultaneously authentic and staged, realistic and yet entirely manufactured. It is also a work that relies almost entirely upon its visuals, and has no need of dialogue to achieve its dramatic impact.

W. S. Van Dyke's *White Shadows in the South Seas* (1928), on the other hand, was a much more commercial picture from the start and was designed as MGM's first "part-talking" picture, premiering at Grauman's Chinese Theater on August 3, 1928, after considerable location shooting in Tahiti. Once again, Robert Flaherty had been involved in the early stages of the film's production, but as would happen with Murnau on *Tabu,* Flaherty's leisurely style collided with Van Dyke's no-nonsense professionalism, and Flaherty departed the project soon after principal photography commenced. Van Dyke, who later directed *The Thin Man* in 1934 in a mere twelve days, making overnight stars out of Myrna Loy and William Powell, was also responsible for the racist African epic *Trader Horn* (1931), which marked the first time that a Hollywood sound crew had photographed indigenous African tribal life.

Van Dyke's diary of the shooting of *White Shadows in the South Seas* demonstrates that from the start of the shoot, Flaherty and Van Dyke did not see eye to eye about the proper methodology of shooting, the length of the schedule, and the approach to the use of native islanders in the film. Van Dyke, a journeyman director who liked to print the first take on most scenes, preferred to keep the pace moving on the set at a rapid clip and had no patience for Flaherty's ethnographic style of filmmaking, in which the finished work grows organically out of the footage shot, rather than from some artificial structure imposed from without. Indeed, it does seem clear that from the start, the ambitious

Van Dyke sought to take over the sole direction of the film. Initially, MGM, the film's producer, seemed happy with the stylistic dichotomy between the two filmmakers, announcing in the trade paper *Film Daily* on November 6, 1927, well before the start of location photography, that "W. S. Van Dyke will aid in direction. Flaherty will handle all atmosphere shots and direct the expedition, while Van Dyke will be in charge of the dramatic sequences" (qtd. in Behlmer 16).

But on location, as Van Dyke's diary demonstrates, the two men had little affection for each other and rapidly lost any collaborative spirit that they might have had before the production got under way. Filming began on December 10, 1927 (Behlmer 20), and only three days later Van Dyke wrote that "Flaherty gave me heart failure yesterday for a moment or two when he said he would like to live here for the rest of his life" (qtd. in Behlmer 24). While Flaherty was entranced with the ease and relaxation of the South Seas, Van Dyke took a more typically colonialist stance, writing in his journal that "as long as one can kid themselves on South Seas first impression [*sic*], the country is wonderful; but if you get a little analytical, then you begin to appreciate home" (qtd. in Behlmer 25). Van Dyke also saw the natives as potential targets of sexual conquest, but noted that "I am told that the great majority of them are full of syphilis" (qtd. in Behlmer 25), thus putting an end to his dreams of sexual tourism, which seem to have been foremost in his mind, along with a desire for as much liquor as he could possibly imbibe.

By February 7, Van Dyke's campaign to helm the film alone had succeeded. Convincing the MGM brass that Flaherty was impossible to work with, Van Dyke noted triumphantly in his journal that "[I] have been asked to take over the entire company and make all the picture . . . have had to retake all of Flaherty's stuff. It was putrid. Not only does he know nothing about pictures but also nothing of natives" (in Behlmer 46). His pride deeply wounded, Flaherty was forced to stay on the island until a boat arrived in March to take him back to the United States, while Van Dyke reshot the entire film.

Based on a novel by Frederick O'Brien, *White Shadows in the South Seas* chronicles the alcoholic collapse and dissipation of Dr. Matthew Lloyd (Monte Blue), once a respected physician. Having drifted to a Polynesian island, Lloyd is appalled by the nefarious activities of pearl merchant Sebastian (Robert Anderson), who mercilessly exploits the native pearl divers to increase his own wealth. Enraged by Lloyd's interference, Sebastian arranges to have Lloyd falsely convicted for a crime and lashed to the captain's wheel of a boat that is then set adrift on the ocean. The boat is eventually caught up in a huge storm, and Lloyd is shipwrecked on an island where the influence of Europeans is still unknown. The natives treat Lloyd as a deity, and for a time Lloyd regains his faith in life and a sense of hope and purpose in his work. But as the film ends, paradise once again proves to be ephemeral as "civilization's" grasp extends into new territory, and Lloyd's Pacific idyll is brought to an abrupt conclusion.

King Vidor's tragic South Seas romance, *Bird of Paradise* (1932), was remade by Delmer Daves in 1951, in appropriate sumptuous Technicolor. In the original version, as in the remake, a young man (Joel McCrea in the first version, Louis Jourdan in the remake) falls overboard from a passing ship and is rescued by a beautiful Polynesian maiden (Dolores Del Rio in 1932, and Debra Paget in 1951). Unhappily for the lovers, the island's volcano suddenly erupts, and the natives decide that the young woman must be sacrificed to appease the gods. While the conclusion of the film is certainly anything but idyllic, for most of the film, life in the tropics seems like an unending dream; until, as is the theme in many of these films, the influence of Western culture brings about an end to one's reverie. In a similar vein, William Berke's *On the Isle of Samoa* (1950) features Jon Hall as Kenneth Crandall, who escapes after a nightclub robbery with a considerable amount of loot, but after stealing an airplane, crashes on an uncharted island near Samoa. Despite the charms of the beautiful native woman Moana (Susan Cabot), Crandall remains obsessed with returning to the mainland to spend his ill-gotten gains; for Crandall, paradise holds little allure without the ability to regain his consumer status.

Richard Wilson's *Raw Wind in Eden* (1958) provides another vision of an Edenic island paradise, this time populated by Esther Williams and Jeff Chandler. Laura (Esther Williams) is a spoiled high-fashion model whose plane crashes on a small island off the coast of Sardinia, with her playboy friend Wally Drucker (Carlos Thompson) also on board; Mark Moore (a k a Scott Moorehouse, played by Chandler) is a devil-may-care hedonist who is using the island as an escape from the cares of civilization. Though Mark/Scott is pledged to marry Costanza (Rossana Podestà), much to the delight of her father, Urbano (Eduardo De Filippo), Laura soon inserts herself in their island idyll.

Wilson, who would go on to direct the mildly Edenic comedy *Three in the Attic* (1968), in which three young women imprison their mutual swain in a house and repeatedly force him to have sex until he is literally spent, is clearly more interested in the "triangular" aspects of life on a deserted island than anything else. Nevertheless, the film's tacky execution (it was shot on the cheap in Italy and was one of Williams's last projects) suggests a desire to escape from the confines of Hollywood's pervasive gossip machine, as well as the reality of Williams's and Chandler's ebbing careers, and offers the protagonists a moment out of time to dally on the beach of their new island paradise before they are forced to return to civilization.

The English director Val Guest's *Bees in Paradise* (1944) takes a different approach to the concept of an inviolate island paradise. On an island in the South Pacific inhabited only by women, the only means of procreation is to use the services of sailors who are cast ashore on the island after a shipwreck. However, after a two-month period of sexual bliss, the men are forced to commit suicide, until the next shipwrecked sailor comes along. This outrageous and deeply sexist premise makes the film little more than a wartime male fantasy, replete with an endless succession of tiresome musical numbers as well as wholly inappropriate extradiegetic instrumentation. The film is really a diversion for the British wartime public, anxious to escape from the horrors of the war that assaulted them on a daily basis.

Even in the midst of this carnage the Edenic impulse remained strong, as exemplified by Humphrey Jennings's superb documentary *Listen to Britain* (1942), in which scenes of ordinary Britons at work and play during wartime seem to occur in another world, divorced from the toil and pain of the ongoing conflict, if only as a vision of what the fighting is all about: the stakes that have been placed on the table, the importance of the return to the prewar life of comparative serenity. The idyllic Britain depicted in Jennings's film, with its orderly scenes of children at play and women working in factories while they sing the popular songs of the day in unison, is a depiction of a life in harmony, albeit one under constant threat of destruction. Thus, I would argue that the Edenic impulse in the film is so strong, so deeply felt, and so omnipresent, that the film finally projects the inevitable triumph of the domestic paradise it so effectively presents to the viewer.

Indeed, it seems that the lure of paradise is generically inexhaustible; Barry Mahon's *Pagan Island* (1961; a low-budget riff on Murnau and Flaherty's *Tabu* with echoes of Val Guest's *Bees in Paradise*), Philip Leacock's *Tamahine* (1963), and Richard L. Bare's preposterous *I Sailed to Tahiti with an All Girl Crew* (1968) offer a similarly Othered vision of the South Pacific. *Tamahine*, in particular, is a curious film, in which the title character, Tamahine (Nancy Kwan), a young Tahitian girl, is sent to England to live with her uncle Charles Poole (Dennis Price), who is the headmaster of an archetypal British all-male boarding school. When Tamahine arrives at the school, her uninhibited lifestyle is predictably at odds with the severe discipline meted out by her uncle. But Tamahine solves this artificial culture clash by falling in love with Charles's son, Richard (John Fraser). As the film ends, Tamahine convinces both Richard and Charles that British society is inherently corrupt and repressive, and the three return to Tahiti, where Tamahine sets up housekeeping in a thatched cottage complete with luxurious hammocks and palm frond fans, where the three successfully "escape" from the demands of the British social system to become, by their own wish, perpetually contented outcasts. Nor is this even a faintly exhaustive list of similarly "paradisiacal" films; by my own estimate, there are at least some four hundred other films that deal directly or indirectly with the concept of an "island paradise," a new land where one can begin anew, amend old wrongs, and cast off the burdens of the social constructs found in European and American society.

James Michener's novel *Hawaii* was pulpily adapted into *The Hawaiians*, a sprawling saga by director Tom Gries in 1970, depicting the island chain as a site of endless contestation and colonialist exploitation; in 1966 director George Roy Hill had created a similarly sprawling exoticist epic with *Hawaii*, again from Michener's source novel, featuring a cast that was almost exclusively European, including Julie Andrews, Max von Sydow, Gene Hackman, Richard Harris, Carroll O'Connor, and Torin Thatcher. Hill's *Hawaii* chronicles the efforts of straitlaced missionary Abner Hale (Von Sydow) and his wife, Jerusha (Andrews), to "bring the message of Christ" to the unwilling populace, who react to Hale's fire-and-brimstone sermons with predictable distaste and confusion. With a prurient and sensationalist script credited to blacklisted writer Dalton Trumbo and Daniel Taradash, *Hawaii* is a film of aggressive, wearying scope, fatally over length at 189 minutes, and compromised by Hill's indifferent direction. Fred Zinnemann was originally named as director of the film, but after numerous delays Zinnemann walked off the project, thus sealing its fate as an inauthentic and wholly synthetic enterprise.

More successful in capitalizing on our eternal longing for paradise —and providing it in weekly doses—was *Fantasy Island*, the long-running teleseries, which began with a 1977 TV movie and then morphed into a wildly successful franchise for producer Aaron Spelling and ABC, with a total of 154 hour-long episodes produced between January 1978 and July 1984. In both the pilot film and the subsequent series, the mysterious Mr. Roarke (Ricardo Montalban) and his assistant Tattoo (Hervé Villechaize) are the proprietors of an island where visitors are allowed to live out their dreams and, not incidentally, exorcise various personal demons—but only if they have the $50,000 admission price. Thus, a parade of well-to-do, conspicuously consumerist supplicants constitute the island's continually changing population, as personified by such "B" list celebrities as Bill Bixby, Sandra Dee, Peter Lawford, Dick Sargent, Tina Sinatra, and Carol Lynley.

In its embrace of consumption and reckless luxury, *Fantasy Island* sells the message that paradise, and renewal, can be purchased—for a steep price. In its own fictive way, *Fantasy* Island gestures toward such recent hypercapitalist "reality shows" as *The Swan*, where women are offered a complete body makeover in hopes of securing new self-esteem and social respect, and *Extreme Makeover: Home Edition*, which shamelessly exploits human suffering as an excuse to destroy an existing house and replace it with a luxurious palace with custom-built "theme" bedrooms, sunken pools, and miniature golf courses. *Fantasy Island's* participants often discovered to their dismay that their dream existences (reuniting with old lovers, getting the chance to pilot a fighter jet, being a professional athlete for a day) failed to satisfy, leaving them emptier than before, which is precisely what contemporary television wishes to do (to encourage more consumption). Perhaps the troubled denizens of *Fantasy Island* would have found more respite from their cares on *Gilligan's Island*, where, for four years (1964–1967) Gilligan, the Skipper, and the other stereotypical castaways seemed quite content to submit to the whims of fate and remained peacefully marooned on "an uncharted desert isle" with little, if any, outside interference.

So what, after due consideration, can we learn from all this? Simply that for every paradise, there is a zone of captivity to match it; for every sacred moment, there is an antithetical moment of profanation. To escape implies captivity, and as the narratives discussed in this chapter make abundantly clear, any escape that one might effect is mediated by the notion of return to one's point of origin. Even though most of us are tied by economic necessity to jobs, schools, corporate institutions, and the like, the notion of escape from the daily grind is, in fact, one of our primary objectives when we perform the act of work. To get away, even for a few days, is the unspoken ambition of the average worker—to leave one's job and relax in a safe place where others will care for our needs. But these "others" require payment, and eventually we will have exhausted our "time out of time" and be forced to return to the jobs that made our marginal freedom possible.

What is also worth noting is that in most fictional accounts of escape, it is the tropics that have the greatest hold on our imagination. In such a tranquil climate, who needs clothes, as some of the quasi-ethnographic films discussed in this chapter readily attest? Food can be had by simply reaching up to grab a banana, or sticking a spear in the ocean to capture a fish, or drilling a hole in a coconut for the sweet milk inside. While most cinematic visions of tropical escape are temporary, there are some films that end with the notion of the islands as a permanent haven: Tyrone Power returning to his mate who awaits him on a tropical island at the conclusion of John Cromwell's *Son of Fury* (1942); Peter Sellers continuing to ply his criminal ways on a desert isle in Cliff Owen's comedy *The Wrong Arm of the Law* (1963); Adrian Edmondson and Rik Mayall comfortably ensconced on a beach of brilliant white sand at the end of Edmondson's *Guest House Paradiso* (1999). In each of these films, society has been judged and found severely wanting, and thus the narratives allow the protagonists a chance for a new existence. But, sadly, these endings are much like the "happily ever after" conclusion of fairy tales, the heterotopic romance novels of Barbara Cartland and her colleagues, and the appalling films of Garry Marshall, particularly *Pretty Woman* (1990), in which a prostitute (Julia Roberts) finds the love of her life with a millionaire "John" (Richard Gere). The true conclusion to all these narratives exists after the fade-out, when the actual work of living remains to be accomplished.

In 1959 the immensely rich Huntington Hartford purchased a "nearly deserted island" for $11 million, promptly renamed it Paradise Island, and then created "a lavish 52-room hotel which looked out on a terraced garden modeled on Versailles. [Hartford] spent some $20 million on the surrounding resort, importing a 12th-century French cloister, constructing a golf course, and building the . . . Café Martinique, whose bathroom fixtures were plated with gold" (Andrews 302). Unlike the average daydreamer, Hartford had no need of a virtual paradise as posited in either the escapist mainstream cinema or, hypothetically, in the works of a performance artist like Janice Kerbel, creator of a nonexistent Shangri-La. Hartford dubbed his resort the Ocean Club, but it began losing money immediately because Hartford had neglected to negotiate one crucial aspect of his island paradise: a gambling license. Without it, the lure of sand, sun, and surf was insufficient to lure the high rollers necessary to maintain the island, and Hartford was eventually forced to sell out his interest in a $30 million investment for little more than $1 million (Andrews 302). Hartford tried to extend his Utopian vision into the artistic community, opening the Gallery of Modern Art in Manhattan to showcase his collection of "realistic art," which closed in the 1970s after losing $7.4 million; founding *Show* magazine, which lasted several years before folding with an $8 million loss; and sponsoring an artists' colony in Los Angeles to encourage young artists, which was eventually lost to creditors as well (Andrews 302).

The world that Hartford sought to create required constant infusions of cash to remain even tangentially solvent; when Hartford's resources were depleted, his Utopian empire collapsed. In the same fashion, the all-inclusive resort holiday so popular today because it offers the concept of a "gated" Eden—in resorts such as Sandals—has a definite start and end date attached. The return to the real is implied by each act of ritual abandonment; although we don't wish to admit it, back home the e-mail, phone messages, and bills are piling up. To completely disconnect from the world for an extended period in today's society is a luxury afforded to only the very few, while the rest of the populace seems contented by the thought of "lottery luxury," in which a TV host will appear at their door to whisk them away from their ordinary lives. A popular television program, *Wife Swap*, offers bored housewives the opportunity to "change husbands" for two weeks. For the first week, the visiting wife must abide by a book of rules left by the wife she is "replacing"; in the second week of the swap, the visiting wife gets to impose her will on her temporary husband and children. By picking couples with distinctly oppositional lifestyles (a family who works out at the gym three hours a day swaps wives with a sedentary family addicted to fast food and nonstop television viewing), the show manages to generate a certain artificial frisson. But the real impact of the show is minuscule; despite the use of predictable stereotypes, MTV editing patterns, and comic sound effects to enhance the absurdity of the situation, *Wife Swap*, like all supposed reality programs, is highly choreographed toward a specific end. Each of these shows offers the participants the chance to escape from their lives, in exchange for cash or travel, if they are willing to submit to hypersurveillant documentation and editorial humiliation after the fact. The real experience of their "time-out," in fact, is obliterated by the final construct of the show. Nothing has really been exchanged, except for the viewer, who has allowed his or her time to be subsumed by an artificial spectacle of social manipulation while being bombarded with advertisements for a wide variety of products and services that are, for the most part, nonessential indulgences.

And even if one does permanently change one's location, who is to say that Eden might not change as a result of a new social influx and become much like the place that had been abandoned? As Alexandra Hudson noted near the end of 2004, Berlin is undergoing a peculiar phenomenon in which those who fled to the West after the fall of the Berlin Wall are now becoming nostalgic for their former place of residence. Germany has been unified, and the Eastern and Western portions of Berlin are now merely geographic designations, not political zones, but for some, the Edenic move to the West has not been all that satisfying.

In this case, Eden has clearly failed those who believed in it, despite the momentary glow following the collapse of the Soviet regime. Indeed, the signs are everywhere that the same regime may well be on the way to reification. Vladimir Putin has expressed interest in serving beyond his proscribed term as president if he feels that it is the will of the people; as a former KGB agent intimately familiar with the methods used by the Stasi, Putin probably detects in this wave of nostalgia for the Iron Curtain a desire to be dominated, to be controlled, to be part of a larger, more unified whole. Secession is not always the answer, nor is it often even desirable. And yet, as a quick tour of the Web makes transparently clear, there is no shortage of people who feel that all their problems could be solved if they could simply move to a desert island, abandon their present mode of existence, and begin anew: the ultimate escape.

In late 2004 a widely televised credit-card advertisement offered one lucky winner precisely this dream of "freedom"; their own island, to do with as they see fit! In ads promoting the contest, the lucky male winner lies on a beach of glistening white sand, sporting a long beard, gesturing desperately to a rescue helicopter for assistance. But when the helicopter lands, and two concerned medics rush to his aid, the man jumps to his feet, shouts "Gotcha!" and asks his wife, who is hidden in the bushes near by, whether or not she has captured his prank with her camera. No need to worry about plumbing, sanitation, farming, electricity, communication with the outside world, medical care, or any of the other quotidian concerns of contemporary society. You have your own island! Surely, this should be sufficient to fulfill your most grandiose dreams of escape.

In October of 2004, one Prince Lazarus Long announced the creation of "The Principality of New Utopia," an autonomous city-state on a tropical island in the Caribbean, modeled after the writings of novelist Ayn Rand, motivational speaker Napoleon Hill, science-fiction author Robert Heinlein, self-help guru Dale Carnegie, and economist Adam Smith. Based on a political platform that deifies individual "entrepreneurship," New Utopia will offer "Charter Citizens" the ability "to negotiate exclusive licenses" for the first "boat dealer, or hardware store, tobacco and drug wholesaler" on the island, and touts itself as "an ideal system of opportunity and rewards for achievers," favoring "free wheeling, capitalistic, laissez-faire economics" as a basis of trade. The principality also plans to offer "the most advanced and progressive medical center in the world, planned to surpass even the standards of the Mayo Clinic," as well as "the ultimate luxury spa," and a casino "modeled after the opulent edifice in Monte Carlo, Monaco" (Principality of New Utopia Website).

Raising the $350 million necessary to get the New Utopia off the ground is being done via the Internet, where Charter Citizenships are offered to the public at large. The new nation, which will be located, if all goes well, "115 miles to the west of the Cayman Islands in the Caribbean," promises to be a tax haven for the wealthy, actively seeking those who feel disenfranchised under the economic systems of their home countries. Whether or not the Principality of New Utopia ever gets off the drawing board may be a matter of discussion, but one thing is certain. In designing a capitalist paradise for the wealthy and privileged, Prince Lazarus has created a peculiar sort of Eden, in which commerce and hypercapitalism are the touchstones of success. This is a long way from the dreams John Pierson and his family had when they adopted the 180 Meridian Cinema in Fiji, an adventure that has now been transformed into a documentary entitled *Reel Paradise,* directed by Steve James, which premiered at the Sundance Film Festival on January 22, 2005. As Pierson noted, he and his family stayed in the tropics for about

> 18 months. I started going in and out of the country about 6 months before my whole family came. It was a once-in-a-lifetime memorable experience. Which is not to say that it was all great, because when you go somewhere that you fall in love with it's always great at first, but once you stay there long enough life is the same anywhere on the planet, you're going to have conflicts with people and troubles you have to overcome, and Fiji was no exception. But showing movies there for free about four days a week, it was just about the greatest experience you could have in your life if you care about film. The people just loving the movies so much because there were no other competing forms of entertainment. Movies were it. Go to church, go to the theater, that was it. ("John Pierson Interview")

James's film about Pierson's Fiji experience is rough, raw, and offers a much more realistic vision of life in the islands than most conventional Hollywood product. In mainstream cinema, however, Bruce Brown's *The Endless Summer* (1966) and William Asher's *Beach Party* series offered a conveniently packaged and endlessly recyclable vision of paradise, one that would captivate a generation of younger viewers, and this sort of film is the focus of the next chapter.

CHAPTER TWO

Eternal Summer

It was American International Pictures who first isolated the teenage viewer from the rest of the members of the typical American household and (astonishingly) targeted the summer as a prime season for filmgoing, while the majors in the early-to-mid-1950s still viewed the June through August date span as "dead time." Everyone was on vacation; surely no one would want to go to the movies. Founded by James H. Nicholson and Samuel Z. Arkoff in 1954 as American Releasing Corporation, AIP changed all that, beginning in 1954 with John Ireland's *The Fast and the Furious* (since remade three times), followed by a series of program Westerns, albeit with a feminist edge, directed by AIP's most prolific auteur, Roger Corman: *Apache Woman* (1955), *Five Guns West* (1955), *Gunslinger* (1956), and *The Oklahoma Woman* (1956). But these projects gestured toward the past more than the future; Westerns had been a cinematic staple since Edwin S. Porter's *The Great Train Robbery* (1903).

But AIP soon realized that these "B" Westerns weren't going to significantly advance their fledgling corporation, and so they hit upon two key strategies that would guide them through their early years as a production entity. First, they would control both halves of the double bill by producing two modestly budgeted films simultaneously and sending them out as an inseparable unit; this assured that

AIP received the entire weekly box-office take in each theater that ran their films. Second, they invented the concept of saturation booking, opening a film everywhere at once on the same day with a splashy advertising campaign using radio and TV spots, a practice unheard of at the time. AIP's motive behind the saturation booking process was to get as much out of their films as possible before negative word-of-mouth set in; today, the practice has become routine in an effort to avoid piracy, eliminate the competition, and forestall lukewarm critical and audience reception. As Robert L. Ottoson details,

> AIP's early films were created in an interesting fashion. Nicholson would conjure up a title, e.g., *The Beast with 1,000,000 Eyes* [David Kramarsky, 1956], and develop an advertising plan around it. After this was done, the screenplay would be written and the film quickly produced. Among independents AIP was one of the first to offer saturation bookings. Such films as [Edward L. Cahn's] *Dragstrip Girl* [1957] and [Herbert L. Strock's] *I Was a Teenage Frankenstein* [1957] would be teamed up with thematically related features and play in four or five dozen theaters in an urban location split almost equally among drive-ins and indoor theaters. Since these exploitation films supposedly did not have any redeeming characteristics, they were shown for only a week or two but would always garner a profitable economic return. Arkoff and Nicholson catered to the same audience that larger companies, which produce such films as [those in the . . .] *Friday the 13th* [series] do now—primarily the high school and college-aged youths who are looking for some cheap thrills with their dates on a Friday or Saturday night. . . .
>
> Beginning in 1963 the beach-party-type films solidified AIP's reputation as being the supreme producer of youth exploitation films. Unlike other youth-oriented films, these particular ones always eliminated the young people's parents. This surf-and-sand crowd seemed to exist in a sort of nether world where they never went home. . . . Young people were . . . shown as . . . existing

> in a hermetically sealed world where all they had to worry about was a bad sunburn. (xii–xiii)

These films promised (and delivered) an endless world of sun, surf, and innocent pleasure, along with a complete absence of responsibility. Beginning with William Asher's *Beach Party* (1963), "the film that started the trend of having American teenagers believe they were ersatz Californians" (Ottoson 87), the AIP *Beach Party* cycle went on to include Asher's *Bikini Beach* and *Muscle Beach Party* (both 1964), as well as Don Weis's *Pajama Party* (1964), Asher's *Beach Blanket Bingo* and *How to Stuff a Wild Bikini* (both 1965), Alan Rafkin's *Ski Party* (1965), transporting the *Beach Party* ethos to the ski slopes, and Weis's *The Ghost in the Invisible Bikini* (1966). With this last entry the series collapsed at the box office, as teenagers became embroiled in the war in Vietnam, the draft (which directly affected AIP's target audience), and the "Summer of Love" phenomenon, which manifested itself in such later AIP efforts as Corman's *The Trip* and Arthur Dreifuss's *Riot on Sunset Strip* (both 1967). As Richard Staehling wrote about the AIP *Beach Party* series,

> William Asher, the director of . . . *Beach Party, Muscle Beach Party, Bikini Beach,* was once asked about the company's shift from gang wars to beach bashes: "Our audiences welcome clean sex," said Asher. "They are bored with juvenile delinquency." It was hardly a revelation, but Asher was right. The press had abandoned delinquency as one of its favorite subjects by 1958, and was off covering phone-booth packing and leisure living in California. Delinquency ceased to be a marketable commodity. No one wanted to watch mayhem in the city ghettos when they could watch the same thing at Malibu Beach. . . . The first one off the American-International assembly line was *Beach Party* with Annette Funicello and Frankie Avalon. . . . The budget was considerably larger than anything done in the black-and-white, leather jacket days (*Bikini Beach* cost $600,000, a far cry from the $100,000 or so put out for something like *Dragstrip Girl*) and it

reaped proportionally larger profits. . . . [No] one smoked, drank, or touched each other (except in volleyball). "They're what I want my son to be at their age," said director Asher.

[AIP tackled the *Beach Party* series with such] overzealous enthusiasm that the genre became a dull stereotype within one year, and a lifeless cadaver in two. The surf scene fell victim to the fastest and most thorough exploitation campaign ever conceived, and although such films were produced well into the mid-1960s, anything made after 1964 is merely an epitaph for an already long-departed genre. No matter really, for even if AIP had been more prudent in exploiting the magic of the West Coast beaches, Frankie and Annette would have still hit the skids in 1964; that was the year the Beatles really arrived. (236–238)

5. Annette Funicello and friends survey the scene in William Asher's *Beach Party* (1963). Photograph courtesy of The Jerry Ohlinger Archives.

The collapse of the *Beach Party* films was a matter of cyclic inevitability for producer Arkoff, who noted in a 1974 interview that

> [y]ou always have to be concerned about competition, any time you start something new. And we have been innovators. Nobody was able to compete with us on the beach pictures. The other companies saw they were successful, that they should make some but they didn't understand the fundamentals. We had no parents or serious adults in any of our beach pictures. The adults were comic: Buddy Hackett, Don Rickles, Keenan Wynn. Once the others started to compete, they used adults. One company made one and called it *For Those Who Think Young* [Leslie Martinson, 1964]—the old Pepsi-Cola slogan. That is the most ridiculous, hidebound, stupid concept I can think of. To put a middle-aged slogan on a youth picture. What kid would go to see a picture called *For Those Who Think Young*? (qtd. in Strawn 265)

The *Beach Party* pictures thus represented a moment out of time, a fantasy world constructed for kids who were stuck at home in the Midwest or other isolated areas, forced to perform daily chores around the house, take out the trash, and deal with the exigencies of teenage life in their relations with their town, their parents, and high school culture. For teenagers of the early 1960s, caught between the end of the Elvis era in rock and roll and the drab conformity of the Eisenhower years on the one hand, and the looming threat of Vietnam as well as the promise of social revolution presented by the Diggers, hippies, and other fringe social movements on the other, the *Beach Party* films represented a kind of Heaven, a place where anything was possible. As Gary Morris perceptively noted in his essay "Beyond the Beach," the *Beach Party* films

> have a schizoid air, typical of the period of social flux in which they were made. While the "text" . . . is a farcical portrayal of the carefree lives of happy vacationing teens experiencing minor

romantic problems, the subtext is *reassurance.* The films exist in an insular world untroubled by the Cold War (fear of nuclear holocaust), collapsing race relations, exploding criminality and drug use, the sexual revolution, and the emerging Vietnam War. They show teenagers as wistful, comic, conformist creatures, sexless and predictable, ultimately willing to carry on the traditions of consumer capitalism that they, as voracious consumers themselves, clearly benefit from. . . .

Consequently, the beach movies could hardly help being reactionary, as they presented AIP's now sugarcoated vision of the coming generation, to assure mainstream society that, in spite of mild personal eccentricities like surfing or falling in love with mermaids (*Beach Blanket Bingo*), young people were ultimately predictable and trustworthy and would fall in line. The major conflict in these films is between DeeDee's (Annette Funicello) middle-class values (yearning to get married) and Frankie's (Frankie Avalon) wanderlust, expressed as an inability to commit himself when tempted by "the Big Wave." The films thus exist far from the headlines of the day, in a never-never land of white leisure-class youth, reaping the postwar profits of their parents' hard work and studious conformity to enjoy the pure sensations of innocent irresponsibility (however brief) and sanitized romance. Blacks do not exist in the world of the films, with the exception of the traditionally acceptable role of guest star: Stevie Wonder in *Bikini Beach.* You'd never dream there was a massive civil rights struggle occurring in the culture at large. And isn't that the point of the films? The offscreen space, the world beyond the beach, is a terrifying reality that must not be allowed to intrude.

Yet, while AIP and Asher had created a successful fantasy formula in the *Beach Party* films (Asher wrote most of the screenplays for the early films in the series, as well as directed them, as a sort of "working vacation" from his job as director of the TV series *Bewitched,* starring

Asher's then-wife Elizabeth Montgomery), it was a concept based on a genuine phenomenon of the era: surf culture. Pop groups such as the Beach Boys and Jan and Dean, along with the Surfaris, the Hondells, Dick Dale and His Del-Tones, and numerous other musical aggregations ruled the AM radio Top 40, which in this more Edenic time was dominated by sixties pop music, much of it dedicated to genuine social change, as in the music of Bob Dylan, Barry McGuire, P. F. Sloan, and the later compositions of the Beatles and the Rolling Stones. What AIP did, then, was to capture the essence of a lifestyle and then market it to the populace at large, most of whom had never surfed or even seen a beach in their brief lifespans.

AIP's example was, naturally, copied by the other Hollywood studios, but never with the same degree of self-referentiality. Sidney Miller's *Get Yourself a College Girl* (1964) slams Mary Ann Mobley, Chad Everett, Nancy Sinatra, and Willard Waterman (as the buffoonish adult figure of authority), along with the Dave Clark Five, Astrud Gilberto, the Animals, Stan Getz, and the Standells into an eighty-six-minute mélange of sex, music, and portentous moralizing at an isolated yet luxurious ski resort; as with the AIP films, there is no concern for time, money, or any of the other circumstances of actual existence. William Witney's *The Girls on the Beach* (1965) sticks closer to the AIP formula (the film's working title was *Summer of* '64), and showcases the Beach Boys, Lesley Gore, and the Crickets (the late Buddy Holly's back-up group) in a Spring Break fantasy that, curiously enough, centers on the *non*appearance of the Beatles. When John, Paul, George, and Ringo fail to materialize, the film's cast attempts to impersonate them, with predictably disastrous results. And yet there is a haunting scene in the film in which Beach Boy Brian Wilson sings a gentle ballad around an improvised campfire on the beach, recalling the innocence of the era, and the title song's promise of sexual license ("the girls on the beach / are all within reach / if you know what to do") is Edenically mediated by the overwhelming chasteness of the film's obviously hasty execution.

Don Taylor's *Ride the Wild Surf* (1964, with an uncredited directorial assist from horror specialist William Castle) stars Fabian, Peter Brown, and Tab Hunter as three surfers who visit the island of Oahu in search of the "last wave" of the season, and soon become romantically involved with Shelley Fabares (late of *The Donna Reed Show*), Susan Hart (Nicholson, wife of the late James H. Nicholson of AIP, and a regular in the AIP beach pictures until coproducer Sam Arkoff decreed that her appearance in AIP films constituted "nepotism"), and *I Dream of Jeannie*'s Barbara Eden. The entire film is suffused with the warmth of the gorgeous location shooting by the gifted Joseph Biroc; the film's title song is performed by Jan and Dean, and became a Top 40 hit shortly after the film's release. In a sense, *Ride the Wild Surf* is one of the most "authentic" of the 1960s surf films, if only by virtue of its Hawaiian locale and the copious amounts of actual surfing footage used in the film (when Frankie and Annette went surfing in the AIP films, it was always through the courtesy of some convenient rear projection). Lenny Weinrib's *Beach Ball* (1965), produced by AIP but released by Paramount, uses a nonstandard AIP cast (Edd "Kookie" Byrnes, Chris Noel, Robert Logan, Aron Kincaid, and Gale Gilmore) in a gender-bending comedy that resembles nothing so much as a poor man's *Some Like It Hot* (Billy Wilder, 1959). With Dick (Edd Byrnes) as their leader, a trio of musicians resorts to anything to redeem their instruments from a pawnshop—including dressing up as women to win a "battle of the bands" contest. The Righteous Brothers, the Four Seasons, and the Supremes lend musical support in what is even by the most modest standards a deeply formulaic film. Nor does the list stop there. Other AIP-styled knockoffs of the period include Maury Dexter's *Surf Party* (1964), Weinrib's *Wild, Wild Winter* and *Out of Sight* (both 1966), and Dexter's *Wild on the Beach* (1965). This is just a partial catalogue of the numerous films inspired by the AIP series; clearly, Asher and AIP had created a subgenre in 1960s cinema, specifically attached to a certain time and place.

Yet one should also consider the interesting and socially disruptive case of Stephanie Rothman's *It's a Bikini World* (shot in 1965, released in 1967), which is arguably the first feminist surf film, a precursor to more recent films in the genre such as John Stockwell's *Blue Crush* (2002), in which a group of young women compete to win a surfing contest. Rothman's sun, sand, and surf film is infinitely more innocent than *Blue Crush,* which depicts the rough-and-tumble world of competitive surfing with considerable fidelity. Yet at the same time, Rothman had the dubious distinction of being the only working female director in Hollywood at that time other than Ida Lupino, as Henry Jenkins notes in an essay on Rothman's films. Rothman broke into films by working for Roger Corman, then extremely active as a producer of movies for drive-in theaters, who has always been known, even in the 1960s, for giving women a shot within his organization as producers, writers, and directors. As Jenkins recounts,

> A graduate of the University of Southern California cinema program, Rothman was one of a number of "film school brats" hired by Roger Corman to make low-budget exploitation films. Starting as a personal assistant to Corman, she became one of the core directors for New World Productions and later helped to establish her own production company, Dimension Pictures. Her independently produced films largely follow the conventions of the exploitation genres at New World. Unlike many of the other male directors who worked under Corman's production supervision, such as Francis Ford Coppola, Peter Bogdanovich, Martin Scorsese, Jonathan Demme, Ron Howard, John Sayles, James Cameron, Jonathan Kaplan, and Joe Dante, Rothman was never able to move into mainstream Hollywood filmmaking. She left the movie industry following the collapse of Dimension Pictures [which was later absorbed into Miramax as its low-budget horror film brand] and has not made films since.

This makes the fate of Rothman's film all the more poignant; although *It's a Bikini World* follows the rules of the subgenre created by Asher, the script, written by Rothman and her husband, Charles S. Swartz, takes a much more interesting angle on the 1960s surf scene. Delilah Dawes

(Deborah Walley) is visiting her friends in Southern California and is immediately hit on by the egotistical and charismatic Mike Samson (Tommy Kirk). The other women on the beach think Mike is "dreamy," but Delilah rejects his advances, telling a friend that she prefers more "intellectual, even klutzy guys." Mike overhears this and creates a fictitious brother, Herbert Samson, complete with glasses and a nerdy clip-on bow tie, who successfully woos Delilah by reading the collected works of Alexander Graham Bell.

Rothman's film enthusiastically partakes of the pop-culture vision of the era; faux Warhol paintings adorn the walls of Mike/Herbert's "beach pad," and Rothman uses a glossy, pop-eyed cinematic style reminiscent of Richard Lester's 1964 paean to the Beatles, *A Hard Day's Night,* or his surreal comedy short *The Running Jumping & Standing Still Film* (1959), with cartoon balloons for character dialogue, speeded-up action for the comedy sequences, and a final athletic contest between Delilah and Mike that intercuts surfing contests with camel races, skateboarding, car racing, and cross-country running, showing a Monty Pythonesque flair for the absurd. Not surprisingly in Rothman's world, it is Delilah who finally wins the contest, not Mike, in contrast to any of Asher's beach party films, where the women do little more than stand around and cheer their men on or serve as visual decoration.

Rothman's film, far from objectifying women, posits a world of cheerful indolence in which men and women are equally engaged in the pursuit of pleasure alone, divorced from the cares of the working world. No one here will ever grow up, or pursue a career, or accept any responsibility other than keeping their surfboard waxed and knowing the latest pop music (Rothman's film contains fine performances from the Animals, the Castaways, and the Gentrys, among other pop groups). And, as Jenkins notes, Rothman's film contains a much more open attitude toward sexuality than those of Asher; in fact, Rothman herself has complained that "I'm very tired of the whole tradition in Western art in which women are always presented nude and men aren't. I'm not going to dress women and undress men—that would be a form of tortured vengeance. But I am certainly going to undress men, and the result is probably a more healthy environment because one group of people presenting another in a vulnerable, weaker, more servile position is always distorted" (qtd. in Jenkins).

Indeed, Jenkins argues that Rothman's filmmaking (in particular her later, more violent exploitation films such as *Terminal Island* (1973), a decidedly dystopic vision of the future) has a definite political agenda, one that can easily be accessed by the discerning viewer, while general audience members can simply follow the film's narrative, perhaps unaware of Rothman's true vision. Notes Jenkins, "Rothman's politics are nowhere more utopian than when they deal with the erotic material that is at the heart of the exploitation film. . . . Rothman's engagement with the exploitation genres was a tactical one; she agrees to follow certain formulas and produce certain images, in order to gain access to systems of production, distribution, and exhibition."

Rothman's other films include *The Velvet Vampire* (1971), *Group Marriage* (1973), and *The Working Girls* (1974). *The Velvet Vampire* was perhaps her most famous film, being a reworking of Sheridan LeFanu's *Carmilla*, the archetypal lesbian vampire tale. It is sad that Rothman's vision was never fully assimilated into the industry as a member of the "Corman generation." Her works are fresh, sharply observed, and technically accomplished; one can only speculate that it was sexism that ended her career as a filmmaker. Yet her works are revered by a number of contemporary cineastes, and Rothman's unique vision of the 1960s and early 1970s was an inspiration for the new wave of women filmmakers who came to prominence in the 1980s and beyond. Rothman was a maverick, using the hypercommercial cinema to advance her personal vision. *It's a Bikini World* gives us a tantalizing peek at what might have been a less sexist and more egalitarian genre, in which women and men at play exist as equals, rather than rivals.

Yet beyond this commercial vision of the lure of the beach, a loosely knit group of maverick filmmakers was creating authentic documents of the era, on minimal budgets, that preserve the raw authenticity of the California surf scene in the late 1950s and early 1960s. As an essay on surfing in the journal *Hemispheres* notes, the sport has had a long and varied history, rising and falling with the tides of colonial intervention. In an anonymous essay entitled "Surfing History," the author notes that

> By the time of the first recorded European visit to Hawaii in 1779, surfing was deeply rooted in centuries of Hawaiian legend and culture. Chiefs demonstrated their ocean-taming prowess at their own beaches, using olo boards (as long as 24 feet) riding waves prone or standing up. Commoners surfed at different beaches and had to content themselves with shorter boards. Legendary surfing incidents inspired place names, and the kahuna (experts) created chants to bless their new surfboards, bringing good fortune to the man or woman riding it. With the rise of European influence and the arrival of Christian missionaries through the 1800s, surfing declined and nearly disappeared for 150 years. In the early 1900s, however, surfing made a remarkable comeback, and in the 1960s the sport became a full-fledged industry. (117)

This twentieth-century renaissance was documented in the works of a handful of dedicated surf enthusiasts. Certainly the most famous of these renegade filmmakers is Bruce Brown, whose crossover hit *The Endless Summer* (1966), originally intended solely for an audience of fellow surfers, eventually emerged as an independently produced commercial film. Brown conceived *The Endless Summer* as a twist on the usual surfing documentary of the era, in which "two surfers . . . would take advantage of the fact that when it was winter in the Northern Hemisphere, it was summer in the Southern. The concept was simple and profound—[by traveling around the globe with the changing seasons] you could live in a surfer's paradise, an endless summer" (Kampion, "Bruce Brown"). The film was shot on 16mm Ektachrome color-reversal film—standard practice for 1960s experimental filmmakers—rather than professional-gauge 35mm film.

The Endless Summer has no plot, and needs none. Rather, it is structured as a Homeric quest for the "perfect wave," as Brown hit the road with surfing buddies Mike Hynson and Robert August, filming on location in "Senegal, Ghana, Nigeria, South Africa, Australia, New Zealand, Tahiti, Hawaii and California" (Kampion, "Endless Summer"). Brown shot most of the film with a spring-wound Bolex camera, another popular tool for independent cineastes in the 1960s; the camera's rugged construction and simplicity of use made it a popular choice for the budget-conscious filmmaker. The spring-wound mechanism meant that there was never any need for electrical power to shoot; 90 percent of *The Endless Summer* was filmed using available light rather than artificial illumination, further simplifying the shooting process. Shot on 100-foot rolls of film, mounted on daylight spools, which ran about two and three-quarter minutes each, *The Endless Summer* is essentially a silent film, without any naturally synchronized sounds. As was the custom with fan-based surf films of the era, the sound track consisted of a mildly percussive surf music score (in this case by the Sandals, a local California surf group), and Brown's off-screen commentary.

The film is essentially a travelogue, structured without much preplanning; Mike and Robert are fixated on their quest for the best surf, and, as in the *Beach Party* movies, there is no sex, little narrative cohesion, and no mention of money, poverty, or racism (especially notable during the South African sequences). Brown simply sets up his camera on a tripod to record the two young men's exploits, intercut, from time to time, with some clumsy comedy segues that help to bridge the gaps between the disparate sequences. What is most striking about *The Endless Summer* is its inherent artlessness. Brown's narration is low-key and unintrusive, the Sandals' score is omnipresent but never overpowering, and Brown favors long takes, uninterrupted by intrusive editing, to document his protagonists' journey. When Mike and Robert finally discover their "perfect wave" at Cape St. Francis in South Africa, the film comes to a gently satisfying conclusion. The odyssey has been successful; now it is time to return home.

6. Surfing as sport and spectacle in Bruce Brown's *The Endless Summer* (1966). Photograph courtesy of The Jerry Ohlinger Archives.

Getting the film before the public at large was another matter. The local Californian members of the surfing fraternity (the film's sexism is also notable; there are very few women surfers in the films, and they are invariably referred to as "girls" and judged only "pretty good" in the skills by Brown's narration) received *The Endless Summer* enthusiastically, but Brown wanted a national audience for this, his sixth feature-length documentary. Sensing that Middle America would be hungry for a taste of sand and surf, Brown and his partner Paul Allen ran *The Endless Summer* in a theater in Wichita, Kansas, for two weeks to packed houses, but mainstream distributors dismissed the experiment as a fluke (Kampion, "Endless Summer"). It was only when Brown and Allen took a gamble and "four-walled" the Kipps Bay Theater on Manhattan's East Side ("four-walling" means renting a theater outright for a flat sum; the filmmaker is then allowed to keep the entire box-office receipts, with no percentage being owed to the exhibitor) at considerable expense, hoping the New York critics would be favorably impressed by his modest film. As Drew Kampion described it,

> Brown charmed the bored Big Apple critics at a preview screening, telling them he'd paid a hundred bucks for the room, so he expected good reviews. He got them, and the rest is history. "For some reason," says Brown, "the real entrenched film critics seemed to like it, maybe because it was different from what they were used to seeing. We weren't one of them, so a lot of the media in New York were into helping us out, not hurting us. If they did a review and wrote, 'Brown did a shitty movie,' we'd have been dead. But nobody knew who I was, and maybe they felt it wasn't worth criticizing, so they pretty much gave us good reviews and helped us out." (Kampion, "Endless Summer")

The film, which had cost a mere $50,000 to make, was blown up to 35mm, acquired by Cinema 5 for national distribution, and became an international success, as well as spawning an iconic poster (Mike and Robert with their surfboards, silhouetted against the setting sun on a pristine white sand beach) and a successful sound-track album. The film also brought surfing to a wider, receptive audience and legitimized what had been an "outlaw" sport. As Kampion notes appreciatively,

> Prior to 1964, the media saw surfers as rebellious thugs, and Hollywood made them out to be a bunch of idiots. Filmmaker Bruce Brown single-handedly changed that with *The Endless Summer.* It portrayed the wave as a kind of Holy Grail and surfers as knights on a quest. In one stroke, he replaced Hollywood's

> buffoonery with the popular mythology that endures today. *The Endless Summer* was Brown's sixth surfing film in a career that started almost accidentally and proceeded according to the guerrilla template of the times—shoot all winter, edit in the spring, run your ass off all summer showing the damn thing (including doing your own live narration) in school auditoriums and small halls, then pack up for another winter on the road and do it all over again. With *The Endless Summer,* Brown broke that mold. (Kampion, "Bruce Brown")

It had been a long journey from the margins. Born December 1, 1937, in San Francisco, Brown spent his childhood in Southern California, starting to surf at age eleven (in 1948, long before the sport had developed major national attention) at Alamitos Bay. Graduating from Wilson High School in 1955, Brown, who noted wryly that he "majored in not going to school," soon enlisted in the navy, went to submarine academy, and wound up being posted in Hawaii, where he surfed Ala Moana in the mid-1950s with the ultimately tragic figure of José Angel and began shooting 8mm movies of his exploits. Discharged from the navy in 1957, Brown was back in California working as a lifeguard when surfboard manufacturer Dale Velzy offered Brown $5,000 to produce a film that would promote the Velzy surf team. In 1957, as Brown recalled, the $5,000 "covered the cost of the camera, travel and a year's living expenses" (Kampion, "Bruce Brown").

Of this early effort, *Slippery When Wet* (1958), one of the first surfing documentaries made, Brown later recalled that

> It was the summer of 1958. I was a 20-year-old lifeguard in San Clemente, California, which to date is the only real job I've ever held. At nights I worked as a glorified janitor at Dale Velzy's surf shop. Occasionally, while I swept up, Dale would show an 8mm surf film I'd made while stationed on a submarine in Hawaii. He charged 25 cents, and on a big night we'd rake in as much as six dollars.

> Dale, however, being one of surfing's great characters, envisioned bigger and better things for me. We spent the summer negotiating about making a "real" (16mm) surf film. He'd pay for it and I would make it. Eventually Velzy put up $5,000, which was to include, among other things, camera equipment, 50 rolls of film, six plane tickets to Hawaii and my living expenses until the film was completed. I looked for some surfers who not only wanted a free plane ticket to Hawaii, but who could afford to pay their own expenses once there.
>
> I found Del Cannon, an old friend; Henry Ford and Freddy Pfhaler, two well-known surfers from the South Bay; Kemp Aaberg, a hot, up-and-comer; and Dick Thomas, who was the only one of us old enough to have an ID. We boarded the plane for the 12-hour flight to Hawaii which gave me plenty of time to read my book, *How to Make a Movie.* Remember *Slippery When Wet* is 42 years old—it was my first film—I was only 20 years old—so gimme a break! (Brown, "Slippery When Wet")

The film boasted a smooth sound track by West Coast jazzman Bud Shank, and despite his modest budget, Brown's cinematography more than lives up to the task of capturing the spirit of adventure inherent in the film's production.

By 1960's *Barefoot Adventure,* Brown was an established fixture on the surf film circuit along with such early pioneers as Bud Browne (creator of *Hawaiian Surfing Movie* [1953] as well as *Surfing in Hawaii* and *The Big Surf* [both 1957]) and John Severson (whose films include *Surf* [1957], *Surf Safari* [1958–1959], and *Surf Fever* [1960]). Severson also founded *Surfer,* the most successful magazine in the early days of the sport. While Bruce Brown was perhaps the most commercially astute of this early group of renegade cineastes, Bud Browne was arguably the most prolific producer of surf films, with some twenty productions to his credit as well as contributions to the films of others (Borte, "Bud Browne"). Browne was also one of the first to use the music of local surf-guitar legend Dick Dale as a backing track for his documentaries, and many surf historians consider his matter-of-factly titled *Hawaiian Surfing Movie* (1953) to be the first commercially exhibited surf film (Borte, "Bud Browne").

But with widespread publicity the sport boomed, and the beaches became more crowded, polluted, and open to commercial exploitation. Bruce Brown and his compatriots started out as filmmakers simply as a way of supporting themselves as full-time surfers, long before the sport became the institutionalized "thrill-ride" that it is today. With its emphasis on "killer waves" and impossible stunt work, what was once a relatively gentle sport has metamorphosed into an episode of the television "reality" show *Fear Factor*, pursuing the deadliest, fastest, most overpowering surf to pump up the jaded adrenal glands of contemporary audiences. Indeed, many of these proven surfers suffered when they tried to push the sport to its limits. José Angel favored the biggest possible waves and savored "wipeouts" (when the surfer topples from the board during a ride) as part of the fun of the sport. He also liked to "free dive," routinely plunging more than two hundred feet into the ocean without scuba gear. In 1974 his deep-sea diving caused a severe case of the bends and partially paralyzed his right leg. On July 24, 1976, his surfing ability impaired by his injury, José Angel attempted a "free dive" of more than three hundred feet and never returned to the surface (Borte, "José Angel"). Thus, Angel died the death of one who is most at peace when engaged in perilous play, as if to prove to himself and the world that his spirit, if not his body, was essentially inviolable. He became emblematic of the reckless abandon of the early days of the sport, when surfing wasn't a multimillion-dollar business but rather a private pursuit known only to a dedicated band of restless enthusiasts. John Severson's 1970 film *Pacific Vibrations* is essentially an elegy to the lost paradise of surfing in the 1950s and 1960s. As he noted in an interview when the film was released in July of that year, "perhaps what started out as a very personal statement about surfers and their harmony with the earth will remain just that. But it is more important that [surfers] wake up before there is no place left for anyone to surf, or enjoy the simple beauty of a breaking wave" (Kampion, "John Severson").

As for Bruce Brown, the success of *The Endless Summer* was bittersweet. As Drew Kampion recounts,

> After *The Endless Summer*, Brown built new offices in Dana Point, California, and went to work on a film about his other passion—dirt bikes. The resulting documentary, co-produced by his friend the actor Steve McQueen, earned *On Any Sunday* (1971) an Academy Award nomination.
>
> Never much drawn to cities or even crowded theaters, Brown moved his family (wife Pat and kids Dana, Wade and Nancy) to a remote ranch north of Santa Barbara around 1980. There Brown surfed, rode his motorcycles, built a house, got into car restoration, raced sprint cars around his track and, more recently, got into rally cars—an all-wheel-drive turbo-charged Mazda that he and Pat co-race. "We try to stay upright as much as possible," he says.
>
> Brown came out of retirement in 1992 to go on surfari making the Hollywood-sequel *Endless Summer II* (released in 1994 by New Line Cinema), a reprise of the original with Robert "Wingnut" Weaver and Pat O'Connell leading the search. But Brown was disappointed with the process and the result. "I never made any money, except what they paid me to direct it," he says, adding that they basically ignored him once the film was done. "They got bought out by Ted Turner and kind of lost interest in our little product. It was kind of unpleasant, more like a battle than cooperation." (Kampion, "Bruce Brown")

Today Brown supervises the rerelease of his films on DVD and races cars. He hasn't surfed in a while. The moment has passed, and with it, the chance to record authentic moments of the post–World War II American surfing era. Yet the pull of nostalgia remains strong. In 1987

Lyndall Hobbs directed *Back to the Beach*, an affectionate homage to the *Beach Party* series, featuring the series' two key stars, Frankie Avalon and Annette Funicello, along with Connie Stevens, Bob Denver, and Pee-Wee Herman. The film has an undeniably sad air about it, a sense of paradise lost. As Gary Morris astutely notes, "*Back to the Beach* gives the curious effect of looking into a kind of cinematic retirement home, with the exhaustion of now-parents Annette and [Frankie], forced in the earlier films to carry a social burden they could hardly sustain, quite evident. The mindless fun is still there but only in pastiche. The twisting teens have become tired, fretting, middle-class drudges—their parents." But the final nail in the coffin was yet to come. The last vestiges of the original *Beach Party* series were neatly put to rest in Charles Busch's play *Psycho Beach Party*, which was filmed by director Robert Lee King in 2000, combining the "slasher" film of the 1990s with AIP's *Beach Party* milieu. And yet, from the ashes of this seemingly terminal parody (much like Charles Barton's *Abbott and Costello Meet Frankenstein* [1948], which effectively signaled the end of the original Universal horror cycle) the beach film rose again in John Stockwell's *Blue Crush* (2002), a fiercely feminist surfing film with superb location photography that nevertheless failed to catch on with audiences, perhaps because of the film's overreliance on digital special effects to enhance the waves during the action sequences. For all their gentle naïveté, Bruce Brown's films are essentially "raw" documents, undoctored records of events and places that have now passed into the realm of myth and memory. The very primitiveness of Brown's 16mm Bolex camera assured that his films would retain a certain veracity missing in today's digitized cinema, in which the line between the real and the manufactured has been essentially erased.

The vision of sun, sand, and surf was intrinsic to the United States, and it also represented what Foucault might have called a "limit experience." Once you got to the West Coast you simply couldn't go any further, and thus the idea of conquering the sea itself was the next logical step. California popular culture, too, has traditionally been a site of extreme modes of social discourse, and it was in the early 1960s that such culture-challenging figures as Ed "Big Daddy" Roth, with his monster T-shirts and souped-up cars, as well as surf music and early modes of extreme surfing, first grabbed hold of the public's imagination. Oddly enough, surf music was immediately big in Britain, particularly in the provinces, where the nearest surf was to be found pounding against the rocks of Dover, or at Land's End, both treacherous locations for surfing, to say the least. But surf music, which predated Beatlemania and the music of the Rolling Stones, the Pretty Things, and other 1960s British bands, spoke to British youth culture of rebellion and questioned the much-decayed dominant social order of the period, when working-class families went on seaside holidays at rundown resorts like Brighton as their ultimate form of Edenic escape.

What youth in Britain were looking for, in essence, was a site for their own performative escape from tradition, and they found it in the poorer areas of London. As late as 1968 I was able to find lodgings for a month in a beautiful top-floor flat in Islington, on Hungerford Road, for the princely sum of three pounds a week, and thus partake of the tidal wave of bands, happenings, light shows, film screenings, concerts, poetry readings, and other cultural events of the time. If California represented, both spiritually and physically, the absolute limits of pop culture in the United States during the 1960s, then London, with its vast sprawl of cheap flats and raw warehouse space represented a similarly welcoming staging area for the new cultural revolution that dominated most of that decade; a call to engage in the politics of creation rather than possession, a call for an end to racism and sexism, and the beginnings of a social movement that would have a profound effect on both countries as they strove to return to their humanistic roots.

In England the 1960s seemed divided into two distinct periods: Beatlemania in the early 1960s and, as the decade progressed,

Alternative London. Emblematic of London during its early "swinging" period are Richard Lester's two films with the Beatles, *A Hard Day's Night* (1964) and *Help!* (1965), with a plethora of imitators such as James H. Hill's *Seaside Swingers* (1965), with short-lived pop sensation Freddie and the Dreamers; Lester's brilliant and disturbing sex comedy *The Knack . . . and How to Get It* (1965), in which the sexually rapacious Tolen (Ray Brooks) coaches his shy landlord Colin (Michael Crawford) in the "proper manner" of seducing a naïve young woman, Nancy Jones (Rita Tushingham); Roy Boulting's *The Family Way* (1966), starring Hayley Mills, Hywel Bennett, and Murray Head in a finely rendered study of the problems of two newlyweds, with a cheerfully lilting symphonic score by Paul McCartney (his first venture into conventional cinema music); Desmond Davis's *Smashing Time* (1967), with Rita Tushingham and Lynn Redgrave loose in a fantastic "mod" London that has long since ceased to exist; Saul Swimmer's *Mrs. Brown, You've Got a Lovely Daughter* (1968), featuring Herman's Hermits in a throwaway slice of London nostalgia; and Jonathan Miller's *Take a Girl Like You* (1970), in which Hayley Mills tries to preserve her virginity until her wedding night while perennial rake Oliver Reed and Noël Harrison (Rex Harrison's son in real life, and badly underused in the cinema) relentlessly pursue her.

All of these films share a common theme in their casual treatment of sexual activity, lack of responsibility, and thoroughgoing hedonism. This Edenic period would eventually collapse in a haze of drugs and violence in Donald Cammell's and Nicholas Roeg's justly notorious *Performance,* shot in 1968 and shelved by the producers, Warner Bros., and then subsequently released with substantial cuts in 1970. In *Performance,* as in Arthur Dreifuss's American-made *The Love-Ins* (1967), which portrays a Timothy Leary clone as a messianic fraud, and Peter Collinson's remarkable and disturbing British film *The Penthouse* (1967), in which a young couple's luxury London flat is invaded by two brutish louts who use mental and physical torture to break down their flawed "relationship," Eden has collapsed, and all that is left is a wilderness of pain.

7. Left to right, Mick Jagger, Anita Pallenberg, and Michèle Breton relax in the bathtub in Donald Cammell and Nicholas Roeg's justly notorious *Performance* (1968). Photograph courtesy of The Jerry Ohlinger Archives.

And yet the loss of Eden is a state from which humankind can recover and renew itself unceasingly, as history clearly demonstrates. Periods of enlightenment are almost inevitably followed by eras of retrenchment in which the ecstatic excesses of the previous "sacred time" are called into question, and even excoriated, by those who would wish a return to a more repressive social structure. Yet, as difficult as they are to endure, these regressive periods never last because they must constantly reify themselves through the use of force, punitive jurisprudence, economic sanctions, and the widespread dissemination of biased information to create a climate of fear in which many will seek a return to older, more familiar political constructs. But such a return is ultimately impossible. We are always moving forward, and the more severe a regime, the more it alienates its most creative citizens. Eventually they will move to overthrow it and regain the freedom that they once enjoyed.

One of the most evocative documents of the 1960s'cultural renaissance in the British cinema is Jonathan Miller's telefilm of Lewis Carroll's *Alice in Wonderland.* Miller had long been an admirer of *Alice in Wonderland,* and finally the playwright Lillian Hellman cornered him at a party in New York and told him that he ought to stop thinking about the project and get on with it. Miller presented the project to the BBC with a projected budget of 28,000 pounds and was surprised when the BBC immediately responded with a counteroffer of 32,000 pounds, a six-week shooting schedule, and a free hand in the creation of the film. Eight weeks later production on the film began in earnest.

The seventy-two-minute film boasts an all-star cast that includes Peter Sellers, Sir Michael Redgrave, Sir John Gielgud, Leo McKern, Peter Cook, and Wilfred Brambell, to name just a few of the many actors who worked in the film for "scale" salary, or roughly 500 pounds each. Shot almost entirely on location in the English countryside in the summer of 1966, *Alice in Wonderland* stars Anne-Marie Mallik as Alice, who drifts off into dreamland and winds up down the rabbit hole searching for a way home. In the spirit of the time, there was no formal script; Miller simply typed out the dialogue from Carroll's book each day and presented it to the cast on the set, and after a few rehearsals they would do a take. Surprisingly, in view of the large cast and the numerous location shoots, the entire production went very smoothly, with Miller usually getting the shot in one take and moving immediately along to the next setup. This was particularly necessary when working with Peter Sellers, who proved as eccentric off the set as on, occasionally holding up the production while he consulted with his astrologer. But despite these few minor problems, Miller later recalled the entire experience as "an enchanted summer, and one of the happiest times of my life" (qtd. in Dixon 1999, 2).

The film has a remarkably lavish look, due to the fact that Miller personally scouted locations up and down the English countryside for weeks before filming began and approved every shooting location. With the cost of the actors' salaries reduced to nearly nothing, Miller was able to hire the superb cinematographer Dick Bush to shoot *Alice in Wonderland* in 35mm black and white, using technology that one usually associates with a theatrical feature film. The BBC lobbied for the use of color videotape rather than film for the project, but Miller vetoed the idea outright; as a result, the visual quality of the piece is stunningly crisp, enhanced by Bush's deep-focus, wide-angle cinematography. The climactic sequence when the Queen of Hearts runs around shouting "Off with her head!" and puts Alice on trial for her imagined insolence was filmed on a specially designed set at Ealing Studios, but for the most part, *Alice in Wonderland* makes locations in the everyday world surreal, producing a realistic document of unreal events. The result is a film that is both intelligent and adult, shot in a dreamy, almost hallucinatory style, in which fantasy and reality are mingled together in a fever dream of adolescence. A final touch to Miller's *Alice in Wonderland* is Ravi Shankar's mesmeric sitar and oboe score, which effectively evokes the colonial past of the British Empire.

From the start Miller determined that the film would be shot with the characters in Victorian dress, on locations from the Victorian era, and that unlike other versions of *Alice in Wonderland*, the film would be made without elaborate costumes to disguise the actors. As he put it, "Why go to all the trouble of getting these famous actors, and then putting masks over their heads?" The decision to shoot in black and white was also essential. As he told me in 1997,

> I was opposed to the use of color in *Alice in Wonderland* because I was trying to re-create a Victorian film, a film of the early cinema, with the effect of Victorian photography. I wasn't trying to re-create the Tenniel drawings [that illustrated the first print editions of *Alice in Wonderland*], because there was no way you could

> do that on film, so I went for a much more naturalistic approach, but I wanted to get the effect of Victorian photographs, the sort of thing that Carroll himself would have taken. I'm still rather opposed to color under those circumstances. Making *Alice in Wonderland* was an absolutely delightful experience, because it wasn't a standard commercial production. I simply called up all my friends in the theater and told each of them that the other was going to do it, and so in the end they all agreed, and the film was, I think, quite successful. (qtd. in Dixon 1999, 2)

In an age where films are increasingly mass-produced and special-effects driven, Miller's vision of Alice's eternal Victorian summer is a welcome reminder that films can be both entertaining and enlightening. As Miller told me,

> I like great simplicity in all my work. I don't like lots and lots of florid detail, and I want my film and video works to be recognized by the audience as theatrical presentations, or constructs, whether one is doing a project for the cinema or for television. It's much better to simplify, always, rather than elaborate. Movies shouldn't be limited to spectacle; they do the simple things so much better. They should try to present real life in the simplest way possible, and be as unpretentious as possible. When they do that, they're successful. Films don't need to cost a fortune to be entertaining. They do need an interior sensibility and intelligence, which is really the most important thing that a film can have. (qtd. in Dixon 1999, 11)

For Miller, what made the experience such a pure and ecstatic occasion was the complete lack of commerciality that surrounded the project; everyone involved was working simply because they believed that the project ought to be made. When Miller ventured into commercial film production with the aforementioned *Take a Girl Like You*, he was much less pleased with both the process and the results, just as Bruce

Brown found that it was impossible to return to *The Endless Summer* with *The Endless Summer II*. In an interview, Miller told me that

> [As] far as I was concerned, *Take a Girl Like You* was such a catastrophe, and I had such a bad experience doing it, working with stars and working with the conventional studio system, that I simply didn't feel inclined to go on in that direction. Nor did I want to go through the labor with studios of 'packaging' projects, putting together this star with that story, getting 'properties,' going to meetings and the like, that I thought it much easier to go on directing plays and operas, and television documentaries. If the system had been more congenial, perhaps it would have turned out differently. (qtd. in Dixon 1999, 5)

Film is inherently expensive; indeed, it is perhaps the costliest medium for any artist to work in. This was not, of course, always the case, especially in experimental films of the 1960s, but when one makes a film with some hope of a commercial return, then the costs mount rapidly. The problem with this is that as expenses increase, one becomes more willing to bend to public opinion rather than to strike out on one's own, and can lose sight of one's own vision. Robert Towne, for example, began working as a scenarist for Roger Corman on *The Last Woman on Earth* (1960), in which, because of budgetary restraints, he also appeared as an actor under the pseudonym of Edward Wain. This modest little film, shot in color and CinemaScope in Puerto Rico in just a few days for less than $100,000, told of a post-Edenic world in which two men compete for the affections of one woman. Corman never had any money for his films; but even though he pushed his cast and crew through impossible schedules on such pre- and post-Edenic films as *Naked Paradise* (1957), *The Saga of the Viking Women and Their Voyage to the Waters of the Great Sea Serpent* (1957), and *She Gods of Shark Reef* (1958), Corman could offer his actors and writers the most precious of creative commodities: total freedom. Working with Corman, Towne was thrown in at the deep end and told to create a screenplay;

when an actor failed to appear, he was pressed into service and turned in a superb performance. In short, he was pushed to his creative limits. Then came Roman Polanski's *Chinatown* (1974), which had a much higher budget and profile, as well as the services of Jack Nicholson (another Corman alumnus) in the lead; the film made Towne's reputation as a writer. But in the years following this success, Towne found that he had trouble working on his own vision within the Hollywood system. After a period in the late 1970s and early 1980s of working on frankly commercial projects (other than his own film *Personal Best* [1982], which was a commercial failure despite excellent reviews), he has of late worked on screenplays for such projects as *Days of Thunder* (1990), *The Firm* (1993), *Mission: Impossible* (1996), and *Mission: Impossible II* (2000). In short, something has been lost. That something is innocence.

In the early days of Andy Warhol's studio, which was first located in an abandoned firehouse, Warhol and his associate Gerard Malanga labored under conditions of absolute poverty to create the work on which the bulk of Warhol's reputation now rests: the *Marilyns, Car Crashes, Electric Chairs, Race Riots*, and other seminal works that created, almost single-handedly, the essence of Pop Art. These early paintings sold for absurdly low sums, often as low as $100 a painting, if one were lucky enough—and prescient enough—to purchase a Warhol canvas in 1963 or 1964. Once the gallery screenings started, that phase of Warhol's career was over and he became a machine, cranking out one silk-screened work after another in his Forty-seventh Street Factory, at ever escalating prices. After his near fatal shooting in 1968, Warhol, working now at his new Factory at 33 Union Square West, concentrated on portraits of the rich and famous not only to pay the rent, but also to disguise the fact that his original inspiration had fled;

he was now, for all intents and purposes, the ghost of a genius. Only in his final days, even though the prices for his works had skyrocketed, did Warhol return to his essence with the *Shadows* series, and his final works, the *Last Supper* paintings, *Skull* paintings, and the *Heaven and Hell Are Just One Breath Away* canvases, which reprinted the covers of apocalyptic religious tracts (for more on Warhol's final works, see Dillenberger). Warhol's work began out of a need to create, out of a raw creative passion, and he surrounded himself with artists, poets, filmmakers, and social mavericks to create the right atmosphere in which to work. But it got lost in the rise to prominence, and commerce replaced art; indeed, it became Warhol's art.

Commerce is never conducive to creation, despite the astronomical values currently assigned to the works of such 1960s artists as Yayoi Kusama, Roy Lichtenstein, Jasper Johns, Edward Kienholz, and others. When works of art from a certain period fetch such inordinately high prices at auction galleries, what is being bought is not so much the work of art itself but rather the memory of its creation, when it was new, both physically and conceptually. As the work's genesis recedes into the past it becomes ever more important to hold onto the work itself, to obtain it, to possess it, to attach to it the moment of its original inception. When one buys a work of contemporary art, one is not only buying the painting, video sculpture, or installation piece itself; one is also buying the work's future, both as a commodity and a totemic reminder of the era in which it was created, and the values that informed that era. When one buys a work with a historical provenance, one is attempting to replicate the past through immediate contact with the work; even being in the presence of the object in question is, oftentimes, sufficient. But the work of the past belongs to the past; the work of the future is being created this moment, and as yet has no assigned value. If it becomes one work in a community of similar creations, or part of a "movement," its value will be immeasurably enhanced. Art redeems us by reminding us of the creative impulse nascent in the very act of existence.

As a site of specific commerce, of substantive investment, the cinema remains the site in which money is most crucial in the creation of a work; it is money that determines the visual sheen, or lack thereof, of any given film. Francis Lawrence's *Constantine* (2005) is a superb example of a seamlessly slick post-post-modern, twenty-first-century entertainment. The lead character, John Constantine, played by the dispassionate Keanu Reeves, strives to keep the forces of evil from breaking forth into the mortal world while the angel Gabriel (Tilda Swinton, in the film's one convincing performance) plays Devil's advocate and seeks to assist in the coming of the Son of Satan. The film's visions of Hell are borrowed from Jean Cocteau's *Orpheus* (*Orphée*, 1949), a ravaged urban wasteland dominated by the ruins of giant buildings, populated by lost souls (in *Constantine*'s case, lost digitally generated souls; real people are so *passé*). *Constantine*'s vision of Heaven is equally derivative, but from a much less distinguished source; Hallmark greeting-card visions of a plasticine paradise await Constantine when he momentarily ascends heavenward at the end of the film only to be pulled back to the bonds of mortal existence at the last possible second. But what is most striking about *Constantine* is the film's pristine emptiness; there is nothing real here, nothing at stake here, no real character development, despite the "world hangs in the balance" exterior motif. The film exists simply to be exploited; it is not meant to accomplish anything other than its own marketing strategy, as if to give the executives responsible for its manufacture a bargaining chip in the international cinematic marketplace. The future of the film is thus easily foretold: with Reeves (the *Matrix* series trailing in his wake), slick production values, the Marvel comics tie-in, bookings in thousands of theaters throughout the world, and given the film's financial pedigree, even if it "fails" at the box office, it will succeed—through foreign, DVD, on-demand, and other marketing strategies. Thus is the future of the work determined solely through its distribution, backing, and casting before it even exists; a project with "lesser" stars will never achieve the same level of financial success, no matter how well it is reviewed. Indeed, reviews have become largely irrelevant. It is entirely a matter of distribution.

In *Performance,* there is no future in the work that ex-pop-star Turner (Mick Jagger) has created; time and value have passed him by. Living in a dilapidated house in a rundown area of London, Turner presides over a peculiar ménage, including Pherber (Anita Pallenberg), Lucy (Michèle Breton), and hoodlum-on-the-run Chas (James Fox). Chas is an expert in destruction—he revels in "decorating" the betting shops, porno theaters, bars, and other shady business enterprises that refuse to pay protection money to his boss, Harry Flowers (Johnny Shannon). But when Chas kills a fellow gangster for revenge, Harry decides that he can easily dispense with Chas's services, and Chas is forced into hiding in Turner's basement. Chas's problem is simple: he likes his work too much. But Turner's problem is more complex; he no longer likes the work that once propelled him to the top of the charts. Taking drugs of various kinds to escape the pain of existence in his tattered domain, Turner exemplifies the fall from Eden into dissolution and despair. When Chas comes into Turner's life unexpectedly, Turner drugs the hoodlum with hallucinogenic mushrooms and momentarily delights in dressing Chas up in a variety of disguises, ostensibly to obtain a camouflaged passport photo but actually to break down the hypermacho gender construct that Chas depends on to define his sexuality. Addicted to prostitutes and sadomasochistic sex, Chas is repulsed when his feminine side emerges under Turner's and Pherber's tutelage. It is at this point that Chas's old associates finally discover his hiding place and confront Chas, now dressed in decidedly androgynous garb as popularized by numerous pop stars of the era. Making no attempt to escape, Chas asks his captors for one last favor —a final chat with Turner. It is only then that, in Turner's bedroom,

Chas responds to Turner's unspoken wish to be murdered and shoots a bullet into the dissipated pop star's brain, killing Turner instantly.

Performance is thus a post-Edenic film, in which the life's work of a performer has failed to save him, or sustain him, after paradise has deserted him. This is a theme that would later be explored in Michael Apted's *Stardust* (1974), which chronicled the rise and fall of a Beatl-esque pop group and its lead singer, played in the film by another pop star, British rocker David Essex. In the next era, the same story of success and failure would be told again in Brian Gibson's often-neglected *Breaking Glass* (1980). Punk songstress Kate, played by musician Hazel O'Connor, starts out as part of a break-all-the-rules punk band but gradually succumbs to the malign influence of corrupt producer Woods (Jon Finch), and shedding her former bandmates, emerges as a "hot" solo act. In the film's horrifying denouement, Kate discovers that she now hates the music that once liberated her, but because of contractual obligations she is still forced to perform it. The film concludes with a concert sequence in which the exhausted Kate, shot up with methamphetamines against her will, screams out her signature pop hit to an audience of fashion slaves who have copied her clothes, coiffure, and gestures, but care nothing about the passion that originally informed her music. In all three films, then, art has failed to transform the artist or allow her/him to transcend her/his surroundings. Accounts must be settled, debts must be discharged, contracts fulfilled, even if hope is gone.

An equally harrowing vision of art as commerce and a necessity of human existence, albeit on a much more rarified musical plane, is offered by the German filmmaker Jean-Marie Straub in *The Chronicle of Anna Magdalena Bach* (*Chronik der Anna Magdalena Bach*, 1968), which Straub made with his partner Danièle Huillet. Straub, one of the most austere and uncompromising filmmakers of the New German Cinema and one of Rainer Werner Fassbinder's mentors, shot *The Chronicle of Anna Magdalena Bach* with very exacting methods. Whenever possible, Straub used actual instruments from the period (Straub went to the considerable trouble of locating musical instruments from Bach's time in various museums and using them in the film); he employed the actual costumes of the period (again, obtained from various archives); he used musicians rather than actors to represent Bach (Gustav Leonhardt), Anna Magdalena (Christiane Lang), and the other members of the cast; he shot on the locations in which the events documented in Bach's life occurred; and he employed a syntactical structure involving a series of lengthy takes that allow us to enter Bach's world as a participant in his (re-created) existence. This pervasive sense of verisimilitude, the result of scrupulous control over the film's mise-en-scène by the director, has, however, the perverse and precisely designated result of "erasing" Straub's presence within the film and allowing Bach's presence to flow out from the screen as a function of the interlocked gaze between spectator/performer. The protagonists of Straub's film,

8. Gustav Leonhardt as J. S. Bach at work in Jean-Marie Straub and Danièle Huillet's *The Chronicle of Anna Magdalena Bach* (1968). Photograph courtesy of The Jerry Ohlinger Archives.

and the various sunlit chambers they inhabit, are part of a reconstituted reality so all-encompassing that it seems to transcend not only the "fourth wall" of the screen but the boundaries of time (which seems suspended) and space (which appears to be infinitely extended beyond the screen out into the auditorium).

It is important to note that the film derives its authority not so much from the look of Straub's performers but rather from the force of Straub's cinematic gaze upon them, in shots of up to seven minutes in duration without a single cut. It is the reflected power of Straub's gaze into Bach's world that holds us in thrall above all other considerations; Straub's film acknowledges its theatricality while simultaneously providing us with a window to the eighteenth century.

The film was almost never made. Straub insisted on using a Mitchell camera to record the film's lengthy takes, and insisted that the film be shot with directly synchronized sound. This was not surprising, given the performing skill of Leonhardt and Lang in the film's two leading roles, not to mention the acoustics of the shooting locations (in many cases, the actual rooms in which Bach performed his work), and the distinctive sound of the period instruments. Amazingly enough, this was a sticking point for Straub's German-Italian co-producers, who had agreed to shoot the film in color but wanted the entire film to be post-synchronized to achieve "studio quality" sound. This, obviously, was counter to Straub's entire project, and thus three days before shooting the film's final financing was still up in the air. At the last moment, Jean-Luc Godard and the German Kuratorium came forward with the necessary funds to shoot the film in black-and-white, with direct sound; with all of the elements in place for the shooting, Straub decided that it was better to shoot the film in monochrome than abandon it altogether (Roud 64).

As Straub described the film's genesis, *The Chronicle of Anna Magdalena Bach* is a film designed from the start to foreground Bach's music, even though, on the film's sound track, the gorgeous harmonies of Bach's compositions are interrupted by voiceovers in which Bach complains that he is being poorly paid and requires a better salary to support his wife and children. As Straub noted,

> The point of departure for our *Chronicle of Anna Magdalena Bach* was the idea of a film in which music would be used—not as accompaniment, nor as commentary—but as raw material. The only real point of reference was the parallel to what Bresson did with a literary text in *Diary of a Country Priest* [1950]. . . . We also wanted to film a love story unlike any other: a woman talking about her husband whom she loved unto his death. That's the story: no biography can be made without an external viewpoint, and here it is the consciousness of Anna Magdalena Bach. (qtd. in Roud 64)

And yet, despite the framing text, the film is still, as Roud notes, "a documentary," in which, insofar as possible, the viewer is placed in Bach's world as an omniscient observer and allowed privileged access to the composer's inner circle of collaborators; the viewer is privy to his working methods, witness to his struggle to create his own interior world despite the indifference of the bureaucratic society that engulfed him.

That the completed film is a gorgeous celebration of Bach's life, in addition to being perhaps the most spiritually faithful filmic biography of an artist ever created, is thus no accident. Although Straub's camera movement is minimal, when his camera executes a tracking shot it is always for a distinct reason. The film's opening take—running a full three minutes—shows Bach at the harpsichord in the music room of the Prince of Anhalt-Cöthen playing "bars 154 to 157 of the Allegro of the 5th Brandenburg Concerto. As he turns the page, the camera pulls back to show the orchestra" (Roud 73), and, not incidentally, the enormous windows in the rear of the chamber, through which the verdant trees of summer are clearly evident. Indeed, nature is important for Straub, and if his film is a documentary of Bach's life, it is also a record of the time in which he lived and the eternal verity of nature's embrace. In one sequence, for instance, the camera simply gazes at a tree in the distance with clouds passing by; Bach's music continues on track as an off-screen accompaniment. Such a direct link to nature is appropriate for a film that is, in Roud's words, "the story of a 'free man,' one of the last figures in the history of German culture . . . in whom there was no divorce between the artist and the intellectual, not the slightest separation between art and life, no conflict between 'sacred' and 'profane' music" (Roud 71).

Straub's film is thus one of the most affecting documents that the cinema has ever produced of the artist as a financial outsider within the world he inhabits. With every waking moment, Bach must take on ever-increasing amounts of work to keep his family solvent and is forced to create compositions at blinding speed to serve the needs of his various employers. There is, indeed, no separation between Bach the artist and Bach the man; they are one, united, continually striving toward perfection, knowing that this is impossible yet working up until the last possible minutes of life to make it so. In the film's final shot, Bach stares out the window of his small house into the distance, having just endured an operation to restore his sight using the most primitive of surgical instruments; in this, his last view of the world, Bach is still seeking to re-create life as he alone sees it, a world of perpetual work, sacrifice, and ultimately grace.

Louis Malle's *May Fools* (*Milou en Mai*, 1990), another film in which nature is foregrounded, is set in France during the events of 1968—which are, however, never shown on screen. Instead of watching riot clubs, tear gas, and barricades, we are given a microcosm of French society in the late 1960s (much as Jean Renoir did for bourgeois French society in the late 1930s with *The Rules of the Game* [*La règle du jeu*, 1939]), centering on a sleepy country estate cared for by Milou (Michel Piccoli), who is devoted to his mother, Madame Vieuzac (Paulette Dubost). But when Milou's mother dies in May 1968, chaos threatens to engulf Milou's relaxed way of life. As scripted by Malle and Jean-

9. Michel Piccoli as Milou (seated, in white hat) presides over an idyllic spring picnic in the French countryside in Louis Malle's *May Fools* (1990). Photograph courtesy of The Jerry Ohlinger Archives.

Claude Carrière, director Luis Buñuel's longtime collaborator, *May Fools* demonstrates that even when Eden seems limitless, its true duration can be measured in the span of one person's life; in this case, that of Milou's mother. As long as Madame Vieuzac's increasingly tenuous hold on life remained, life at the family estate was measured, deliberate, seemingly eternal. Her death has thrown Milou's entire world into a state of flux.

Malle stages the film in a dreamy torpor; though revolution is brewing in Paris, the characters in *May Fools* are far more interested in their own destinies than that of a nation teetering on the brink of anarchy.

The film's original title, *Milou in May* (*Milou en Mai*), is perhaps more indicative of the film's real ambitions than the American release title. Although the student/worker revolt of 1968 keeps threatening to intrude, in the end Malle's film is about Milou, not France, and about his personal crises, not those of the government. Indeed, what little information that comes through to the house is wildly speculative, and rumors soon become "facts" as the various members of the household take measure of their lives.

The same sort of redolent golden splendor also suffuses Jaromil Jireš's decidedly dreamlike Czechoslovakian film *Valerie and Her Week of Wonders* (*Valerie a týden divů*, 1970). Once again the action takes place in the countryside, as Valerie visits her relatives at their turn-of-the-century estate, only to find that they are vampires, engaging in a sort of ecstatic summer orgy into which Valerie will be initiated. *Valerie and Her Week of Wonders* is a deeply eccentric text, infusing a coming-of-age story with Edenic concepts of purity and lust, inclusion and banishment, into a sensuous tapestry in which nothing is as it seems. Written by Jireš, Ester Krumbachová, and Vitezslav Nezval, the film's brevity (a mere seventy-seven minutes) and its seductive mise-en-scène, sumptuously photographed by Jan Curík, make the film seem almost an outlaw project, or as Tanya Krzywinska argues, an act of social criticism designed to "enforce atheism [by embracing] an anti-Catholic stance, particularly in relation to sexual morality." Yet the film's embrace of sexual excess, and the almost fetishistic depiction of bodily fluids, color, light, flesh tones, and gauzy fabrics, bespeaks an atmosphere of absolute sexual license, rather than creating a fantasy world of repression. In many ways, Valerie is very much like Alice in Miller's *Alice in Wonderland*, reacting to the bizarre circumstances that unfold before her.

The film begins with an image of Adam and Eve, as Krzywinska notes, and Valerie is often seen eating apples in close-up, her overripe lips lingering over the succulent fruit with undisguised satisfaction. Thus Valerie provides us with an image of feminine desire before and after the fall of Eden but without the attached blame that Eve shoulders in Western Christian mythology. Instead, Valerie is seen by the film as a giver of life, a force of purity too intense to be corrupted, while her grandmother (Helena Anyzová) becomes a vessel of corruption. As Krzywinska notes, this is a film that is deeply tied to nature at its most gloriously ripe season, summer, and Valerie herself partakes of this lushness with direct and unabashed delight.

Valerie and Her Week of Wonders presents a world in which all is allegory, one's relatives may be vampires, and all authority figures are suspect; in the opening minutes of the film, a "priest" enters Valerie's dazzlingly white bedroom and almost immediately tries to rape her. Valerie extricates herself from the priest's attack but remains justly suspicious of authority for the rest of the film. What protects Valerie, above all other things, is her connection to nature, which preserves her position within the film as a force of hope within a crumbling family structure.

In many ways *Valerie and Her Week of Wonders* can be read as a more sexually explicit vision of the coming-of-age narrative, centering on the freedom of youth, than its numerous American and British counterparts. Valerie emerges triumphant at the end of the film, despite all adult attempts to corrupt her, and the purity and innocence of her metaphoric quest is valorized by the film's ambiguous conclusion, in which all of the film's events are called into question; it may all have been a dream.

Lindsay Anderson's equally surreal *If*. . . (1968) presents a young Malcolm McDowell as Mick Travis, the leader of a surrealistic rebellion at a British public school. As Mick enlists his various classmates in his plot, the world around him becomes increasing fragmented, to the point that it becomes impossible to separate fantasy from reality. *If*. . . is punctuated by sequences that do nothing to advance the narrative, as is *Valerie and Her Week of Wonders*, but that do a great deal to enhance the mood of the piece as a contemplation on the precariousness of youth and the unreliability of one's perceptions in an often deceptive world.

At one point in *If...*, while cleaning up the school's basement as an enforced punishment, Mick and his compatriots come across an ancient chest filled with various human biological specimens neatly preserved in jars of formaldehyde. In Mick's face we can see a sense of wonder as he confronts these embalmed fragments of life that remind him of his own inevitable mortality. In another sequence Mick and his unnamed lover (Christine Noonan) engage in a playful, animalesque flirtation in a roadside café, followed by a victorious romp on Mick's motorbike in the fields outside. In the already highly homoerotic atmosphere of the school, two young men who are sexually attracted to each other are found sleeping peacefully beside each other in the same bed, lost in a reverie of homosocial bonding. At the film's end, Mick and his co-conspirators climb to the top of the school and ritualistically machine-gun the school's alumni during Founder's Day, and the film ends with a close-up of Mick's anguished face, blasting rounds of gunfire at the school's "old boys," a vision of what Mick himself might one day become.

Director Anderson filmed *If...* on location at an actual British public school (although, for obvious reasons, he had a great deal of trouble identifying an institution that would allow the production of such a script on its ground) and used color and black-and-white stock interspersed throughout the film at random intervals to further distance the viewer from the spectacle that s/he is witness to. Further, this displacement of a consistent visual medium (it's not in color, nor is it in monochrome; it's a mixture of both media, switching back and forth for no apparent reason) enforces the artificial, dreamlike quality of the piece, as if we are witnessing a fiction film that is also partly a documentary, as in Straub's *The Chronicle of Anna Magdalena Bach*. Then, too, Anderson uses direct sound throughout the film to further enhance the "realistic" nature of the project's surreal scenario, creating an unusual mix of cinematic reportage and apocalyptic fantasy. Although the film owes an obvious debt to Jean Vigo's anarchist masterpiece *Zero for Conduct* (*Zéro de conduite*, 1933), which uses a French boarding school as the site of a similar rebellion, *If...* is an entirely original work, and arguably Anderson's finest film, in its explication of the mechanics of youthful revolt.

Summer has always been synonymous with freedom and a relaxation of normative social standards. For many it is the time for vacations; for those in academe, the summer months represent an Edenic hiatus during which the normal exigencies of classwork can be momentarily set aside. Much of *If*... takes place in the summer; the trees that surround the boarding school bloom with ferocious assurance, much as in Joseph Losey's *Accident* (1967), which documents the quietly decadent world of Oxford in the 1960s during the height of summer. Summer is, in itself, an excessive season, in which all that has been dormant for the winter springs forth in a riot of color and sensation, a cornucopia of sights and smells. Summer is a time to make love in the fields, a time to take long walks at night on the village green, a time to ride your motorbike through the tall grass, a time in which all is renewed and made young again.

In such films as Delmer Daves's teen romance film *A Summer Place* (1959), Sandra Dee and Troy Donahue fight back against the hypocrisy of their parents during a stay at a summer house on an island off the coast of Maine. In Sidney J. Furie's *The Young Ones* (a k a *It's Wonderful to Be Young*, 1961), British pop star Cliff Richard (as Nicky) and his backing group, the Shadows (as themselves), work together to prevent the destruction of their clubhouse by ruthless impresario Hamilton Black (Robert Morley), who wants the site for a new office building. Unbeknownst to all except Nicky, Hamilton Black is Nicky's father, and so the film becomes a clash between generations with a predictably Edenic ending in which Nicky and his father are reconciled. Clive Donner's *Here We Go Round the Mulberry Bush* (1967) is yet another tale of youthful promiscuity centering on Jamie McGregor's (Barry Evans) sexual exploits as a young rake about town, set to an appropriately trendy musical score by the sixties rock bands Traffic and the Spencer Davis Group. In Daniel Petrie's *The Idol* (1966), ne'er-do-well art student Marco (Michael Parks) is a bad influence on Timothy (John Leyton), the grown son of Carol (Jennifer Jones), a repressed socialite who treats Timothy as a child. With London in full summer bloom as a backdrop, Marco sets about to liberate Timothy from his overprotective mother and simultaneously seduces Carol, humiliating her and demonstrating that she does not control all the events and persons around her.

In this zone of personal freedom, the artificial zones of "high" and "low" art are convincingly banished. There is no difference, really, between the visions of personal and social freedom offered by these admittedly commercial Hollywood films and Bo Widerberg's *Elvira Madigan* (1967), one of the most gorgeous of all films set in the world of

10. Pia Degermark in the title role of Bo Widerberg's *Elvira Madigan* (1967). Photograph courtesy of The Jerry Ohlinger Archives.

eternal summer, which chronicles the doomed romance of Elvira (Pia Degermark) and Sixten Sparre (Thommy Berggren). It is perhaps more relaxed, a trifle less narrative driven than its Hollywood counterparts, but it embraces the Edenic instinct nevertheless. Elvira, a tightrope walker, and Sixten, a lieutenant in the Swedish army, abandon their former lives (he deserts not only his role as a serviceman, but also abandons his wife and children; she quits the circus where her act was a central part of the troupe's spectacle) and embark on a whirlwind romance, which can last only as long as the season itself. Pursued by the authorities, Sixten and Elvira are forced to live hand-to-mouth in increasingly desperate circumstances, as all the while the lush foliage of the countryside serves as an ironic counterpoint to their plight.

At the film's end, both Sixten and Elvira are unwilling to relinquish their newfound freedom, and passion, for a return to the social order they have spurned. With Elvira's consent, Sixten fatally shoots her while she is walking in a meadow and then turns the gun on himself. Eden has proven a deceptive trap for the couple; initially inviting, it has become a world too beautiful to leave, forcing the lovers into a desperate solution. This is the other side of paradise, when the lure of an idyllic world becomes so strong that it is irresistible, no matter what the cost. It is not surprising, then, that all the films discussed in this chapter exist in a zone of perpetual escape, where the sun always shines and winter never comes. Bruce Brown's *Endless Summer* serves as an apt framing metaphor for our discussion here; somewhere in the world, it is always summer. Eden is perpetual and constantly self-renewing, if only we have the resources to live here forever. But it also serves as a warning that an Edenic state is precisely that because it is so difficult to sustain when everyday responsibilities and the cares of human existence constantly threaten to intrude. Eden is a privileged state, a place of grace that is open to only the few, the deserving and the fortunate. Would one wish to live in Eden forever?

CHAPTER THREE

Paradise Now

In the 1960s, when America temporarily returned to its social senses and began to push back the repressive work of the Eisenhower/McCarthy era, there was a veritable outpouring of individual creative activity in all areas—film, dance, sculpture, performance, painting, and literature. We have not seen a decade as fecund as the 1960s in the creation of an entirely new Edenic mode of living since; "codeheads" would argue that the digital revolution has brought about a fundamental shift in human relations akin to that of the 1960s, and in some respects, they are correct. But text messaging, e-mail, videophone calling, and the like essentially separate us from one another, as we use the communication device in question as a shield rather than a connection. If the digital culture demonstrates anything, it is that we are denied direct communication with our friends and associates; we must spend hours staring at a screen in a desperate attempt to "keep in touch."

Simultaneously our own isolation grows more intense as political factions split the country into warring ideological camps that seek not communication but the annihilation of dissent and the elimination of alternative voices. It was not always so, nor will it remain that way in the future. Eventually the hyperconnectivity of the digital era will give rise to a backlash, in which the artificially congruent "whole" of the digital world will be splintered into obsolescence by a humanist revolt against the multimedia conglomerates. As in the 1960s, a new generation will ultimately drop out of the wired world and explore their inner beings, freed from the synthetic televisual constructs and false "connectedness" of their alternative digital beings.

But, as with all revolutions in thought and action, there is usually a long gestation period of subterranean work that precedes the final outburst of communal creative activity that finally commands the public's attention. The most influential theatrical group of the 1960s, the Living Theater, founded by Judith Malina and Julian Beck, can be traced back to New York City in 1943, when the couple first met as teenagers (Biner 19). Born in Kiel, Germany, Malina had been on the stage since the age of two, until her father, a rabbi, wisely recognized that the dawn of Nazism foretold an attempt to destroy Jewish civilization and fled with his family to America (Biner 19). Beck, who was also Jewish, grew up in relative middle-class comfort in Washington Heights, on the Upper West Side of Manhattan (Biner 19).

After their meeting in 1943, the pair rapidly became inseparable and were eventually married in 1948. Plunging into the vital artistic community of post–World War II Manhattan, Malina and Beck began seeing as much theater as they possibly could (often sneaking in during intermissions to avoid the price of a ticket) and talking "incessantly about poetry, theater, painting and literature" (Biner 19). Julian had some initial success as a painter after dropping out of college in 1942; by 1945 he had become part of Peggy Guggenheim's extended circle of artists, mingling with the likes of Jackson Pollock and William Baziotes and exhibiting his work at Peggy Guggenheim's gallery (Biner 20). He survived by doing odd jobs, while Judith began studying with Erwin Piscator in a dramatic workshop at the New School for Social Research and doing occasional bit parts in television dramas, as the new medium was just beginning to flourish in New York and required an extensive corps of players for its mostly live dramas (Biner 21).

But the dream of their own theater, separate from the Broadway empire and working along very different artistic lines, obsessed both Beck and Malina. As Pierre Biner recounts,

> They made their first attempt [to open the Living Theater] in the summer of 1948 in a basement on Wooster Street. The theater was to be maintained on subscriptions. The repertory was to consist of Japanese Noh dramas translated by Ezra Pound, medieval miracle plays, Strindberg's *Spook Sonata,* Ibsen. They rehearsed and sold sixty subscriptions. Then the police came, thinking they had discovered a clandestine whorehouse. The theater on Wooster Street never opened. (21)

For the moment, the dream of the Living Theater was put on hold. But inspired by the strength of their vision, the couple pressed on. By 1947 Malina and Beck were reaching out for support to Jean Cocteau, Paul Goodman, John Cage, and set designer Robert Edmond Jones (Biner 22). Jones advised them to present their works in lofts, galleries, churches, any place they could other than a conventional theater; to create entirely new work, they had to reject the notion of a stable, artificially solid base and bring their work to the world, presenting their productions in any space that came to hand. The first performance by the Living Theater thus took place in the Becks' apartment on August 15, 1951, after nearly a decade of experimentation, arguing, testing, and exploring the limits of what was then known to be theater. The very intimacy of the Becks' small living space added to the immediacy of the experience; the first plays on the bill were *Childish Jokes* by Paul Goodman, *Ladies' Voices* by Gertrude Stein, Brecht's *He Who Says Yes / He Who Says No,* and Lorca's *The Dialogue of the Mannequin and the Young Man.* As Biner noted, "One finds clearly stated in their very first performance what were to be some of the Living Theater's abiding interests: anarchism, poetry, Oriental theater (via Brecht), improvisation, experiments with language" (26).

From this modest beginning, the Becks began to consolidate their connection with their newfound audience. Between 1951 and 1963, when the Becks presented their career-defining production of Kenneth Brown's play *The Brig*, the couple staged twenty-two productions featuring twenty-nine plays in all, including Gertrude Stein's 1938 play *Doctor Faustus Lights the Lights*, which was the first Living Theater production presented at a conventional venue, the Cherry Lane Theater in Greenwich Village, in December 1951. After witnessing a performance, the poet William Carlos Williams was moved to write the Becks a letter which said, in part, "[your production] is so far above the level of commercial theater that I tremble that it might fade and disappear" (qtd. in Biner 29). The subject matter of Stein's play is deeply telling in light of later productions by the Living Theater, which stressed the importance of following the dictates of one's own conscience, despite all outside influence, and had a direct influence on their decision to later perform *The Brig*. As Biner recounts, in Stein's play "Faust's beloved, Marguerite, dies and is sent to Hell. Faust encounters Mephisto and asks him what sin he had to commit in order to join her. The answer is kill. Faust kills a dog and a little boy. Marguerite does not recognize him when he arrives in Hell, for he is not the Faust she had loved" (30). What fascinated the Becks, in particular, was Stein's repetitive, hypnotic language, as exemplified by this incantatory excerpt from scene 1 of Stein's play, in which Faust chants

> I knew it I knew it the electric lights they told me so no dog can know no boy can know I cannot know they cannot know the electric lights they told me so I would not know. (qtd. in Biner 30)

As Julian Beck noted in an interview with Pierre Biner, "Faust is inundated with electric light; it is the price of his soul; in *The Brig* it is the blinding light falling straight from the ceiling on the prisoners of the Marine Corps. Faust asks how he can get to Hell, and he is told: by killing. Hell is the 'brig,' the prison for men who have been taught to kill" (qtd. in Biner 30).

These early productions were subsidized by $6,000 that Julian had inherited from his aunt (Biner 24), but this money was soon exhausted.

In a state of ecstatic desperation, the Becks mounted a production of Gertrude Stein's *Ladies' Voices,* Eliot's *Sweeney Agonistes,* and Pablo Picasso's 1941 playlet *Desire Caught by the Tail* under the umbrella title "An Evening of Bohemian Theater," for a total cost of $35 (Biner 31). The presentation produced the greatest response from the public that the company had yet seen. The Becks were finally able to pay their actors from the box-office proceeds, and the Living Theater became a paying concern, conducted entirely according to their own cultural dictates.

At the same time, as instinctual pacifists the Becks had been participating continuously in demonstrations against the nuclear proliferation that marked the 1950s and 1960s, being arrested on numerous occasions for their activities. By this time the Becks had fully committed themselves to the life of the outlaw artist, as they and their troupe moved from one theater to another, presenting plays they believed in, irrespective of their financial potential, or lack of it. Thus it was when Jack Gelber brought his play *The Connection,* about a group of jazz musicians waiting for a "fix" of heroin, that Julian Beck immediately decided that the company had to produce it, no matter how controversial the subject matter. Gelber was so poor at the time that he could not even afford postage to mail the play to the Becks; instead, he presented it in person, and the Becks accepted it on the spot (Biner 46). The play was first presented at the Living Theater's new facility at Fourteenth Street and Sixth Avenue on July 15, 1959, to immediate critical acclaim; in 1960 the filmmaker Shirley Clarke produced a feature film of the Living Theater's production, although the Becks were dissatisfied with her cinematic translation of the work.

Kenneth Brown's *The Brig* opened at the same theater on May 15, 1963, and was also a commercial and critical success, but the troupe's financial circumstances, always precarious, forced them to leave the Fourteenth Street facility and move the production to the Midway Theater on West Forty-second Street. *The Brig,* depicting one day in a Marine Corps lockup, was a brutal success from the first day of its public presentation. Based on Brown's own experiences in the Marine Corps, the play depicts the dehumanization of those marines who have failed to live up to the military's expectations of them as robotic killing machines. When the play was closed by the Midway Theater management after two additional months, Jonas Mekas, the experimental filmmaker and critic for *The Village Voice*, decided to create a document out of respect to the Becks and shot a film version of *The Brig* in the now-closed theater. As Mekas described the filming,

> I went to see *The Brig*, the play, the night it closed. The Becks were told to shut down and get out. The performance, by this time, was so precisely acted that it moved with the inevitability of life itself. As I watched it I thought: Suppose this was a real brig; suppose I was a newsreel reporter; suppose I got permission from the U.S. Marine Corps to go into one of their brigs and film the goings-on: What a document one could bring to the eyes of humanity! The way *The Brig* was being played now, it was a real brig, as far as I was concerned. . . . Next day I got the film and equipment. The theater was already locked up by the owner. We got the cast and the equipment into the theater through the sidewalk coal chute, late at night. (We left the place the same way at three or four in the morning.) We found part of the sets already taken down. The cast put it all back into place. There was no time for any testing of equipment or lights. The lighting remained the same as during the regular stage performance. I placed two strong floods on the front seats of the theater so I could move freely around without showing the seats. I had three 16mm Auricon cameras (single-system, with sound directly on film) with ten-minute magazines. I kept changing cameras as I went along. The performance was stopped every ten minutes to change cameras, with a few seconds overlap of the action at each start. I shot the play in ten-minute takes, twelve takes in all. (190–191)

The resultant *cri de coeur* won the Grand Prize at the Venice Documentary Festival in 1954 and was a hit of the 1964 London and New York Film Festivals as well. It was described as being "more like a grueling ballet than a story. The way the camera moves becomes a vile replica of the jailers' insatiable physical fascination with the victims. *The Brig* is a horrifying image of degradation, and it works in the cinema with grim brilliance" by the London *Observer* (qtd. in FMC 104). *The Brig* marked a decisive turning point for the Living Theater, despite its enormous commercial and critical success. Stein's play, Gelber's, Brown's—all were visions of what America had become, an inhospitable Hell that attempted to destroy its most influential artists. There was only one route open: escape.

As a result of their defiant refusal to leave their Fourteenth Street facility, where the actors in *The Brig* (before the move to Forty-second Street) staged a sit-in to block IRS agents pursuing the Living Theater for back taxes, and Julian Beck offered the audience a ladder to gain entrance to the theater, the Becks found themselves on trial for "impeding a Federal officer in the pursuit of his duties." At the resulting trial, the Becks chose to defend themselves, rather than relying on court-appointed counsel, hoping to talk to the presiding judge as a fellow human being, with the added moral support of Tennessee Williams and Edward Albee as witnesses for the defense, to no avail. In the course of her testimony to the court, Judith Malina expressed her sorrow at the way in which the United States had become a restrictive and repressive nation, words that have added resonance today, saying in part that

> The Germany in which my father was brought up was a free country but it changed its nature, it changed its laws, and the laws became more and more rigid and the laws no longer left room. . . . I am not suggesting that we have come to such a terrible pass. Pray to God that we never shall. But the rigidity of the law and unwillingness of the law to change and yield to hu-

> man feeling, this seems to me the crucial point at which tyranny begins. (qtd. in Biner 79)

Despite Malina's impassioned eloquence, or perhaps because of it, the Becks were found guilty as charged and given fines and prison sentences. Displaying some leniency, the judge allowed the Becks and their troupe to travel to London to present *The Brig*. While working there, the pair wrote and performed as a group effort *Mysteries and Smaller Pieces* in Paris, Brussels, Basel, Anvers, and Berlin until mid-December 1964, when the Becks were obliged to return to the United States to serve their sentences. Judith reported for her jail sentence at the Passaic County Jail, while Julian was incarcerated at the Danbury Federal Penitentiary. Judith was released on January 13, 1965, while Julian was freed on February 12, 1965, and both immediately returned to Europe and the beginning of exile (Biner 82–84).

Beginning in 1965 the Living Theater became less interested in performing even the most advanced conventional plays and more intrigued by the possibilities of creating an atmosphere of mysticism and self-enlightenment in increasingly direct contact with their audiences. After the *Mysteries* series and productions of Jean Genet's *The Maids*, the group produced a series of highly idiosyncratic versions of *Frankenstein*, *Antigone*, revivals of *The Brig*, and finally, in July 1968, at the Cloîture des Cannes in Avignon, France, as part of the Festival d' Avignon, the first public performances of *Paradise Now* (Biner 243). Composed of a series of "rungs" on the way to paradise, the play begins with direct confrontation with the audience, drawing them into the spectacle that they are witnessing, completely abandoning the centuries-old tradition of the inviolable "fourth wall" that demands that actors refuse to acknowledge their audience, except for brief asides, which serve as exceptions. In the case of *Paradise Now*, the audience is incorporated into the troupe as co-creators of the work. As described by Pierre Biner, the work begins with what the Becks described as "the rite of guerrilla theater":

> While the audience is taking their seats, the actors file silently into the theater. Approaching people here and there, separately, they declare in tones ranging from anguished confidence to neutral objectivity, "I am not allowed to travel without a passport." Whatever the reaction, verbal or otherwise, the actor repeats the sentence without engaging in conversation. The little statement becomes more intense; the actor remains detached from the surrounding people. After about two minutes of this all the actors let out a great shout—releasing, in effect, the mute cry that has welled up within everyone during the foregoing action. . . . When silence is restored, the actors utter another sentence in the same manner: "I don't know how to stop the wars." There is another joint shout; then the statement becomes: "You can't live if you don't have money." The next sentence is: "I am not allowed to smoke marijuana." The last: "I am not allowed to take my clothes off." Here, instead of ending with another yell, the actor angrily undresses in the midst of the audience, taking off as much clothing as the law allows. (182)

This series of incantations is followed by a second section, "The Vision of the Death and Resurrection of the American Indian," in which members of the troupe portray Native Americans being slaughtered from gunfire by soldiers while engaged in a sacred council ritual; then a third segment, "New York City: Eight Million People Are Living in a State of Emergency and Don't Know It," in which audience members are urged to alternately identify with the police and other forces of social repression and then with the spirits of the departed Native Americans, using the chant from R. D. Laing's *The Politics of Experience:* "If I could turn you on / If I could drive you out of your wretched mind / If I could tell you / I would let you know" (qtd. in Biner 186). Subsequent "rungs" in the journey include "The Rite of Prayer," "The Rite of Study," "The Vision of the Creation of Life," and "The Rite of Universal Intercourse," in which members of the troupe "lie off the stage and caress the bodies of those nearest them while the spectators gather around" (Biner 196). The work concludes with "The Rite of the Mysterious Voyage," in which the actors attempt to wrestle with interior forces that compel them toward negative thoughts; "The Vision of the Integration of the Races," which directly confronts the mechanics of racism through the use of a series of oppositional racial epithets; "The Rite of I and Thou," a consideration of human mortality; and "The Vision of Undoing the Myth of Eden," which declares that paradise is within us always, and is the divine state of woman and man, and not subject to the strictures of organized religion. In *Paradise Now*'s final moments, after eight "rungs" of theater/action, the troupe exits into the street with the audience, performers, and audience united as one, marching on the road to paradise.

The impact of *Paradise Now* as a clarion call to the artistic community was intense and immediate. On the negative side, the mayor of Avignon expelled the troupe from the festival and the city, declaring that the performance constituted an "immorality . . . to our youth and our workers" (qtd. in Biner 214). Accordingly, after presenting to the public a manifesto denouncing the provinciality of the Avignon authorities, the troupe presented a free performance of *Paradise Now* near Toulon on August 1, five additional performances of the play in Geneva on August 20–24, and then departed Europe on August 31, 1968, on the SS *Aurelia*, where the group offered an impromptu performance of *Mysteries* in the ship's lounge on September 3. Returning to the United States, the company embarked on a whirlwind series of engagements, presenting *Paradise Now* at Yale University, the Brooklyn Academy of Music, the Fillmore East, NYU at Stony Brook, Rutgers University (where I viewed the troupe in performance and was amazed by their passion, precision, and absolute fearlessness as performers), Bennington College, the Philadelphia YMHA, Cornell University, Hunter College, the First Unitarian Church in Madison, Wisconsin, and even (or perhaps most appropriately) the Soldiers and Sailors Memorial in Kansas City, Kansas (Biner 243–248). After completing a satisfyingly eccentric tour of the United States, the troupe returned to Europe, where fortunately filmmaker Sheldon Rochlin captured an entire performance of *Paradise Now* as a feature-length documentary during one of the troupe's final performances of the work in Brussels in December of 1969, before an enraptured audience of seven thousand people.

What had once been marginalized was now a public phenomenon, embraced by academe, the critics, and general audiences. And yet, with such widespread acclaim, the Living Theater members felt that it was now up to others to carry on the work they had initiated, and gave their last performance as a troupe on January 11, 1970. Later that same month, the troupe issued a manifesto announcing that they were splitting into four separate "cells," one each in Paris, Berlin, London, and India, "to get out of the trap" of being an institution. Further, the document stated

> The Living Theater doesn't want to perform for the privileged elite anymore because all privilege is violence to the underprivileged.
>
> Therefore the Living Theater doesn't want to perform in theater buildings anymore. Get out of the trap; the structure is crumbling.
>
> The Living Theater doesn't want to be an institution anymore. It is out front clear that all institutions are rigid and support the Establishment. After twenty years the structure of the Living Theater [has] become institutionalized. All the institutions are crumbling. The Living Theater [has] to crumble or change its form. (qtd. in Biner 226)

The year 1970 was the cutoff point. The artistic explosion of the 1960s was, on all fronts, retreating. As with all the other manifestations of an Edenic state in this book, paradise was fleeting. And yet, as with the Living Theater, the 1960s in experimental cinema offered an astonishing array of ecstatic visions, which were eagerly embraced by the public. Although in the United States the centers of experimental cinema were confined to New York and San Francisco for the most part, the pre-digital, 16mm culture of the era created a series of film societies throughout the country where local cineastes could gather and bear witness to the cultural revolution that was taking place.

The same cannot be said today. There is little room for playfulness or experimentation in contemporary mainstream filmmaking. The stakes are simply too high; the average feature film costs between $50 and $100 million, and all commercial films must recoup their backers' investment. Thus, the box-office-driven spectacles produced by Hollywood are triumphs of marketing, not imagination. Art-house films and independent films have little hope of finding an audience because of changes in distribution patterns (VHS, DVD, and cable) and the increasing conglomeration of Hollywood. Nevertheless, there is and always has been a body of film art that exists outside the confines of commercial production. Experimental cineastes don't set out to please an audience of marketing executives; they give no thought to the pressures of opening-weekend grosses, nor do they try to manipulate, or even please, the masses. Their films find their own audiences and operate entirely outside of the value system that we have come to know as the Hollywood construct.

In the late 1800s, when the cinema was first invented, filmmakers toyed with the new art form they had created. They hand-cranked the film at variable speeds through the camera and discovered the magic that the cinema had to offer. People and objects could be made to disappear, fly through the air, and change shape at will. Inanimate objects could come to life through the magic of stop-motion animation. Alice Guy Blaché and other early filmmakers experimented with frame-by-frame hand tinting to create color films and experimented with sound; early attempts at sound recording were made using a wax cylinder to synchronize picture and sound.

The Surrealists also stretched the supposed limitations of the new art form, constructing radically inventive editing techniques and ignoring the requirements of conventional narrative to create "cine-poems" of anarchic beauty. Dziga Vertov and his students in the former Soviet Union invented rapid montage editing out of necessity. Denied access to raw stock to shoot new films, they learned how to cut film by re-editing D. W. Griffith's *Birth of a Nation* (1915) in short bursts of hyperedited frames, a style of editing that would become the hallmark of Soviet silent cinema. Experimental filmmakers physically "attacked the film" by scratching it, baking it, dyeing it, using outdated stock—both when economically necessary and by deliberate design—to create a tactile viewing experience that would repeatedly remind the audience throughout the projection that they were witnessing a plastic construct, a creating of light and shadow, in which the syntactical properties of the cinematic medium were always an aesthetic consideration.

Some of the most radical of the 1960s Edenic cineastes included Barbara Rubin, Robert Nelson, Ben Van Meter, Gerard Malanga, Jud Yalkut, and Scott Bartlett. All of these film artists share one thing: a highly personal and deeply felt vision of a new and anarchic way of looking at film and video, fueled by the inexhaustible romanticism of the era and by the fact that film and video were both very "cheap" media in which to work during the 1940s through the 1960s. Film was inexpensive: a 100-foot roll of black-and-white film was $2; color film, $5. Processing cost two or three cents per foot. Filmmakers would often band together to purchase raw stock in bulk, or they would use outdated film that professional companies would simply throw away. Many experimental films were shot completely silent, with sound tracks of music and effects added later.

Although these independent artists screened their films for each other and assisted each other with production chores, each filmmaker was guided solely by her or his own vision, not by the desire to create a film for an audience. Each filmmaker had an individual style and approach to the material that made her or his films uniquely that filmmaker's alone. Thus these films resist categorization and do not fall within the confines of established genres. The independent filmmaker creates films because of an internal drive to do so; the films discussed in this volume are the unique creations of artists who fought to express their vision on the screen, using whatever equipment came to hand, working on nonexistent budgets.

Even in the late 1960s, one could make a 16mm fifteen-minute black-and-white sound film for as little as $200; if one had the desire to do it, anyone could make a film. These filmmakers also disdained, for the most part, the Hollywood model of slick professionalism in lighting, acting, sets, costume design, and other physical production details. The avant-garde filmmakers of the 1920s and 1940s aspired to a certain level of studio gloss in their work, but by the 1950s and 1960s, the Beat and "underground" filmmakers in New York, San Francisco, and Los Angeles were all embracing the idea that avant-garde films should be rough, raw, and imperfect. These were outlaw works, created at the margins of society. It seemed perfectly natural to make a film for oneself as the audience and to ignore both the established film critics and the normal distribution channels. Thus, throughout the history of experimental cinema, various communities developed, each of which provided distribution facilities, screening venues, and the spiritual and financial support necessary to the communal enterprise of filmmaking.

Marie Menken began her career as a filmmaker during World War II, working for the Signal Corps between 1941 and 1945. During her tenure in the military, Menken created and photographed miniature sets for military training films. She also photographed *Geography of the Body* (1943) for her husband, Willard Maas, and created the animated chess sequence for filmmaker Maya Deren's *At Land* (1944). As the fifties progressed, Menken made an entrancing series of short films, including *Hurry! Hurry!* (1957), in which human sperm die in the attempt to replicate human life, set to a sound track of continuous bombing; the lyrical and graceful *Glimpse of the Garden* (1957), in which Menken's camera sweeps through a small backyard garden as if imitating the point of view of a bird, with the sound track of the film comprised solely of continual birdsong; and *Dwightiana* (1959), a brief animated short film in which beads, stones, and other everyday objects take on a life of their own.

Mary Ellen Bute was the first filmmaker to use electronically generated images, utilizing the output of a cathode ray oscilloscope. She named this process "abstronics," which signified a wedding of abstract and electronic forms. Many contemporary developments in computer technology in the cinema represent direct outgrowths of Bute's work. Sara Kathryn Arledge, working on the West Coast in the 1940s, created *Introspection* (1941–1946), an abstract vision of the human body that has much in common with works by Menken and Maas. Arledge's 1958 film *What Is a Man?* is an exploration of the relationships between women and men in life and art. The film presents the viewer with then-revolutionary images of the nude human body as a site of performance and pleasure with a directness that is fresh and original. Arledge was a pioneer in this area, making films that were uncompromising in their graphic nudity, depicting sexuality as a basic human fact rather than relegating physical desire to the pornographic zone of the forbidden. Arledge's work directly tackles the issues of filmed sexual performativity and transcends the mere documentation of human sexuality through the mediation of her humanist gaze. The groundbreaking work done by these filmmakers freed the cinema of many of its imagistic and narrative constraints, but a new wave of filmmakers took this liberating impulse even further in the late 1950s as part of the Beat cinema.

Vernon Zimmerman's satiric *Lemon Hearts* (1960) is a 16mm thirty-minute film produced on the astoundingly low budget of $50 (Sargeant 88). Taylor Mead plays eleven roles in this entirely improvised film, as he drifts aimlessly through the ruins of a series of soon-to-be-demolished Victorian houses, sometimes appearing in drag, sometimes in blue jeans and a sweatshirt. The sound track is once again pirated from jazz records, interspersed with Mead's own Beat poetry ("Oh God, oh God, my feet smell . . . I pissed on Jane Wyman's picture"). With his gracefully languid nymphlike body and a blissfully blank expression, Mead creates the perfect picture of absolute innocence in a hopelessly corrupt universe.

The 1960s are justly celebrated as a veritable renaissance period in experimental cinema, in which some of the most influential avant-garde works were produced. The Kennedy assassination and the advent of the Beatles and the Rolling Stones, together with the influence of such counterculture figures as Allen Ginsberg, Timothy Leary, Lenore Kandel, and Abbie Hoffman, signaled a new openness in American culture. People began to reassess 1950s values, which had once been unquestioningly accepted, and an entire new wave of experimental cinema was born. Filmmakers in the 1960s, working in New York, Los Angeles, and San Francisco, created sophisticated distribution and screening outlets, especially the Film-Makers' Cooperative (a distribution facility) and the Filmmakers' Cinematheque (a film theater, which changed locations numerous times) in New York, and Canyon Cinema in San Francisco. Both the Film-Makers' Cooperative and Canyon Cinema had one guiding principle in their initial bylaws: anyone could become a member simply by placing his or her films in distribution. There was no censorship or "selection" criteria of any kind, and anyone who had a film to screen was welcomed, regardless of the film's content, style, or production values. Thus, Canyon and the Cooperative acknowledged that, above all, the 1960s experimental cinema artist was a free agent, answerable only to her/himself. Previously applied standards were swept away, and an entirely new style of raw, tactile, "funk" filmmaking appeared.

Many mainstream approaches to commercial filmmaking and cinematography would be appropriated from the experimental filmmakers, including light flares, punch holes, leader streaking, and the defiant sloppiness of the 1960s avant-garde, when filmmakers sought to embrace the mistakes in their work and delighted in unexpected superimpositions and the chance manipulations of random editing, echoing the syntactical structures popularized by the composer John Cage and others. In addition, these filmmakers tackled themes of race relations, sexuality, drugs, social conventions, and other topics that the conventional cinema consciously avoided. More than anything else, the experimental cinema of the 1960s was an advocate for social change and complete artistic freedom.

New York animator Robert Breer's works, for example, are elaborately structured free-form affairs that either tease the audience with abstractions that gradually take on recognizable form or assault the audience with a collage of single-frame imagery, in which each image is entirely unrelated to the one preceding or succeeding it. Breer's first film using unrelated, continuous images was *Images by Images I* (1954); a mere ten seconds long, the film is a succession of 240 stills. *Jamestown Baloos* (1957) is a collage film that incorporates seemingly disparate images into a mysteriously coherent whole; *A Man and His Dog Out for Air* (1957) offers the viewer a pulsating, abstract line drawing that momentarily metamorphoses into an image of a man walking his dog at the film's conclusion. *Homage to Jean Tinguely's Homage to New York* (1968) is a document of Jean Tinguely's self-destructing sculpture performance in the garden of the Museum of Modern Art. Breer returned to line animations with *Inner and Outer Space* (1960) and to image-collage films with *Blazes* (1961), *Horse Over Teakettle* (1962), *Pat's Birthday* (1962), *Breathing* (1963), *Fist Fight* (1964), and 66 (1966). Breer's 69 (1969) remains one of the artist's most accomplished works. Basic geometric shapes are rotated against a background of constantly changing colors. As the film progresses, the drawings intertwine, forming new configurations, interspersed with sections of black leader that divide the film into stylistic segments (Renan 129–133).

Storm De Hirsch's *Goodbye in the Mirror* (1964), to pick just one film from her considerable body of work, is a 35mm feature film shot in Rome that deals with the lives of three young American women living abroad. Other De Hirsch films include the brief abstract animation film *Trap Dance* (1968), in which the images are scratched directly onto the film with surgical instruments, and *Shaman: A Tapestry for Sorcerers* (1966), which extends the filmmaker's body into the performance space of the film frame as De Hirsch photographs herself, nude, through a variety of prismatic lenses and diffusion filters, presenting her body to the audience as the site of ritualistic display.

The poet Gerard Malanga, perhaps best known as Andy Warhol's right-hand man during Warhol's most prolific and influential period as a filmmaker and painter, created a series of deeply romantic and poetic films of his own. In them, Malanga's onscreen persona of "the young poet" is foregrounded in each frame. Where Warhol's gaze was clinical and detached, Malanga's extravagant vision bursts forth in such films as *In Search of the Miraculous* (1967), an emotional, vivid poem of adoration for his then-fiancée, Bennedetta Barzini. One of Malanga's most ambitious works, the sixty-minute, split-screen, two-projector, stereo-sound *Pre-Raphaelite Dream* (1968), documents the filmmaker's friends and extended family in Cambridge, Massachusetts, as they perform their lives for the camera.

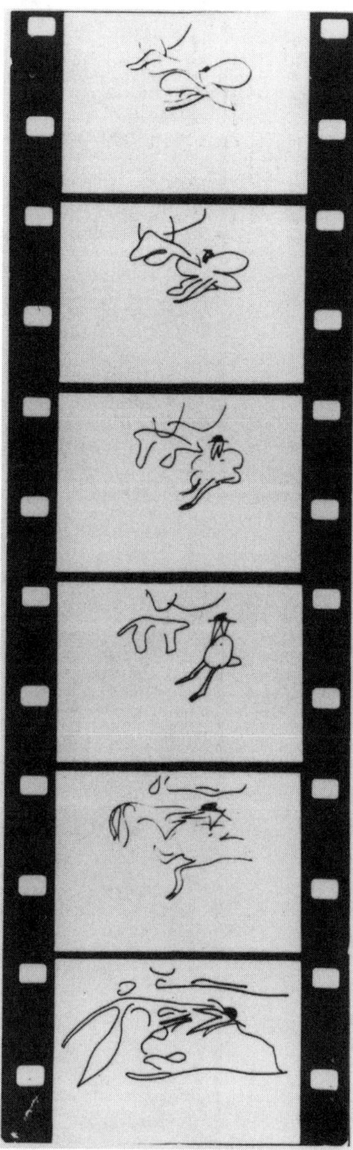

11. Frames from Robert Breer's early animation *A Man and His Dog Out for Air* (1957). Photograph courtesy of Anthology Film Archives.

New Yorker Barbara Rubin's *Christmas on Earth* (1963), created when the filmmaker was only eighteen, is a thirty-minute 16mm double-projection film in which two separate reels of images of the human body in the act of making love are superimposed, one on the other, to create a landscape of desire that remains one of the most audacious cultural statements of

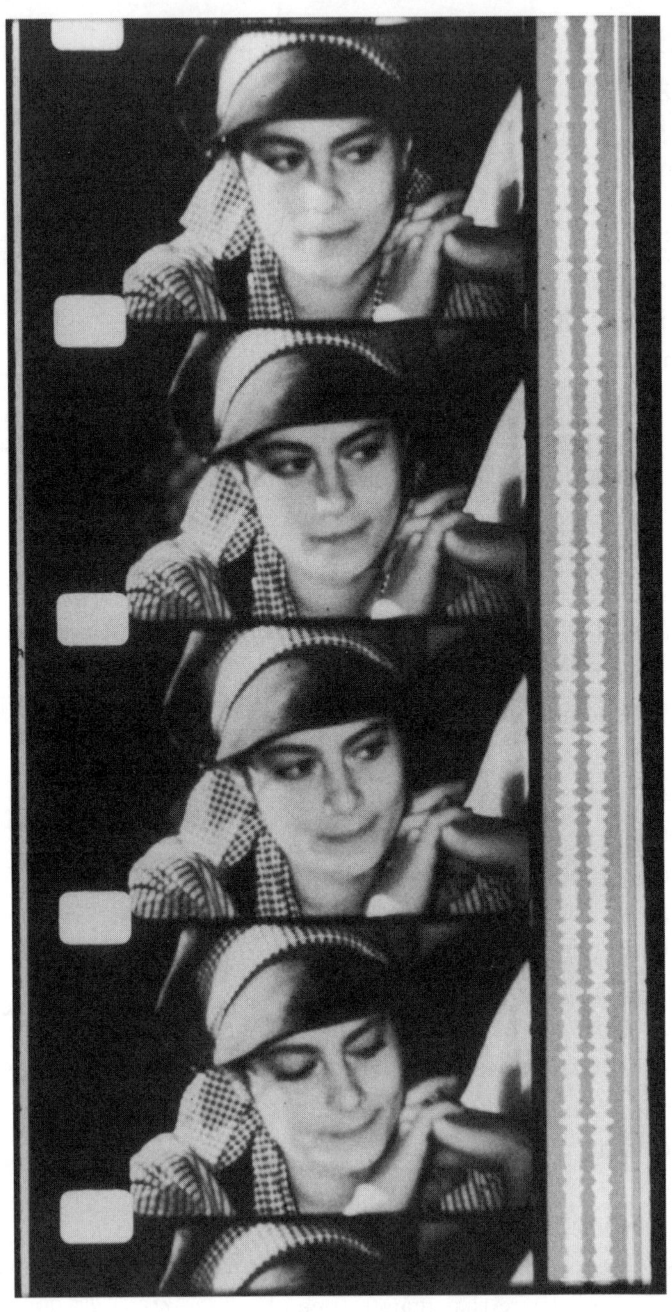

12. Filmstrip of Barbara Rubin, director of the Edenic film *Christmas on Earth* (1963). Photograph courtesy of Anthology Film Archives.

the 1960s. Rubin photographed the images for the film in a free-form, documentary manner and then cut the developed reels of film into short strips, threw them into a basket, and drew the individual shots out one by one, splicing them together in random order. When the film was completed, Rubin instructed the projectionist to run the reels in any order, forward or backward, and to put colored strips of plastic in front of the projector lens at random intervals during screenings of the work (Mekas 174–175).

Jud Yalkut's *Kusama's Self Obliteration* (1967) offers us a vision of the Japanese performance artist Yayoi Kusama engaged in a "self-obliteration" ritual, in which she paints dots of color on leaves, animals, various other objects, and finally on a group of people ecstatically copulating in one of Kusama's endlessly mirrored "Infinity Chambers"; they carry on making love, seemingly oblivious to Kusama's painterly brushstrokes being applied to their naked skin. By linking nature in the form of trees, flowers, grass, and animals to the human experience of performative re/production, Kusama demonstrates that individual identity is mediated by the performative act of "self-obliteration," in which individuality is subsumed in the larger fabric of shared existence.

Stan Vanderbeek's experimental films anticipated many of the techniques we now take for granted in the cinema: computer imagery, the use of specialized projection environments in which to show his films and videotapes, collage animation from newspaper and magazine cutouts (which later became a staple on the Monty Python series), and compilation filmmaking, to name just a few of his contributions to the technological advancement of cinema. Vanderbeek even went so far as to build his own film theater, which he dubbed the "Moviedrome," a spherical structure in the woods near Stony Point, New York, where multiple-projector presentations of his works played for rapt audiences in the 1960s. Vanderbeek's early films include *What Who How* (1957), *Mankinda* (1957), *One* (1957), *Astral Man* (1957), *A la Mode* (1958), *Three-Screen-Scene* (1958), and *Science Friction* (1959), all films using collage cutout techniques to satirize the American consumer dream. *Achoo Mr. Keroochev* (1959) is a two-minute black-and-white sound film lampooning Soviet dictator Nikita Khrushchev: whenever Khrushchev starts to speak during a parade or at the United Nations, he gets hit over the head with a hammer.

In San Francisco, pioneering video and film artist Scott Bartlett created a series of challenging and evocative films in the mid-to-late 1960s, fusing video and film techniques in such early classics as *Metanomen* (1966), *Off/On* (1967), and *Moon 1969* (1969). Often neglected today, Bartlett's work was revolutionary both in style and in content and pushed the limits of film and video in new and often unexpected directions. In *Metanomen* he used black-and-white high-contrast cinematography to create a hauntingly bleak boy-meets-girl anti-narrative set to a sitar sound track. *Off/On*, an abstract, non-narrative cinepoem that is at once haunting and mysteriously seductive, is the first exper-

13. Stan Vanderbeek stands in front of his Moviedrome, a completely enclosed projection space near Stony Point, New York. Photograph courtesy of Anthology Film Archives.

imental film that truly combines film and video imagery in a coherent whole. *Off/On* is for the most part comprised of a series of repeating film and video loops, which Bartlett manipulates through various rephotographing and video colorization techniques to create an intense cybernetic journey that challenges both the physical consciousness and the aesthetic sensibilities of the viewer. In Bartlett's next film, *Moon 1969*, he explores the sensory limits of the viewer: the beginning moves slowly from complete blackness and blankness to glaring white, with aerial footage of an airport runway at night slowly washing in and out. *Moon 1969* proceeds through a series of tempo changes until it reaches stroboscope intensity in its final minutes; the film triumphantly concludes with a long shot of the sun reflected in the sand at the edge of a beach.

Ben Van Meter, a West Coast filmmaker most active in the 1960s, created a gorgeous series of films that celebrate the human body: *The Poon-Tang Trilogy* (1964), *Colorfilm* (1964–1965), *Olds-Mo-Bile* (1965), and his epic *Acid Mantra: Re-Birth of a Nation* (1966–1968), a forty-seven-minute color and black-and-white work of such propulsive energy and intensity that viewing it is almost an exhausting experience. Starting with footage of various rock bands in concert, including the Velvet Underground and the Grateful Dead, the film superimposes as many as ten layers of images simultaneously to engulf the viewer in a cornucopia of sight and sound, all leading up to a climactic orgy during a summer picnic at a party in the Bay Area countryside. As the couples engage in ecstatic sexual unions, Van Meter hand-drips blobs of colored paint directly on the film, as if to suggest the intensity of the energy that is being released by his performers. As the film ends, we see families in the nude, swimming, playing Frisbee, relaxing, and walking in the tall grass.

In all of these films, we see the element of celebration as key to the works' construction. Many of these films, especially Malanga's and Van Meter's, are deliberately anarchic, using over- and underexposure, multiple superimpositions, color and black-and-white film intercut at random intervals, and other aggressive visual strategies to delight and

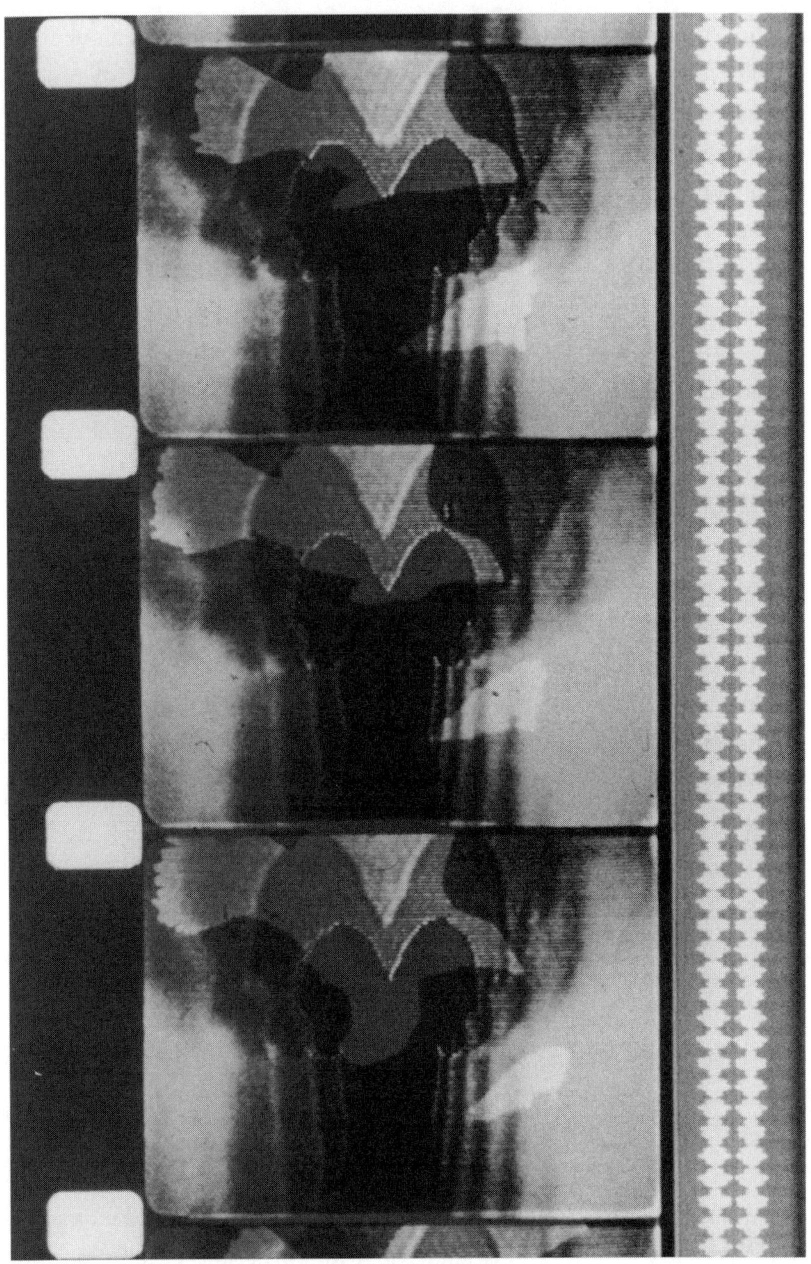

14. Frames from Scott Bartlett's elegiac *Off/On* (1967), one of the first films to fuse the filmed image with video. Photograph courtesy of Anthology Film Archives.

seduce the viewer. In addition, most of these filmmakers, both in New York and in Los Angeles, explored issues of sexuality with a candor that seems revolutionary even today and made their films with a rough-and-ready abandon. In many cases these films were cut in the camera, with not one frame of film wasted in the editing process; the filmmakers would simply string the reels of exposed film together to form a longer work and then present it with an accompanying sound track (Dixon 1998, 48–60).

> In so doing, Van Meter and Malanga were echoing Kerouac's dictum that Time being of the essence in the purity of speech, sketching language is undisturbed flow from the mind of personal secret idea-words, blowing (as per jazz musician) on subject of image . . . Begin not from preconceived idea of what to say about image but from jewel center of interest in subject of image at moment of writing, and write outwards swimming in sea of language to peripheral release and exhaustion—Do not afterthink except for poetic or P.S. reasons. Never afterthink to "improve" or defray impressions, as, the best writing is always the most painful personal wrung-out tossed from cradle warm protective mind— tap from yourself the song of yourself, blow!—now!—your way is your only way. (Kerouac 72–73)

Thus, creation is ecstasy, and the film, piece of music, or written text that results is the purest essence of the self—the most virginal form of self-expression. In Ben Van Meter's brilliant short film *S.F. Trips Festival, An Opening* (1966), the filmmaker captured the essence of the spectacle he was witnessing, in this case, the legendary Trips Festival held in January 1966, aptly described by David E. James as

> an entrepreneurial assembling of previous innovations in mixed media performance, notably Ken Kesey's *Acid Tests.* For each of the festival's three nights, Van Meter exposed the same four 100-foot rolls, sometimes using his hand as a traveling matte and varying

> exposure and focus so that images on each of the three levels of superimposition are continually in the process of emerging from and dissolving back into each other. The spectacular and maximally visual diegesis fabricated in the film is thus a collage, collapsing spatial and temporal distinctions into a continuous perceptual flow that identifies the people in the film with the environment and the event. Personal differences, certainly as constitutive of bounded egos, are subsumed in the synaesthesia of the collectivity in which dancers, musicians, filmmakers, spectators, people of all races—all are performers, permeated by the fractured luminescence of the hall and suffused by the light of old movies, educational slides, and strobe lights that is projected all over its interior. (137)

The sound track that accompanies these images is similarly multilayered and equally dense, in addition to being sped up (as are many of the images in the film) by electronic (for the sounds) or mechanical (for the images) manipulation. Further, Van Meter uses this material right from the camera, without following Kerouac's admonition; although he does trim some of the reels slightly, there are only four or five actual film edits in the completed work. Van Meter's films constitute an image of intertribal harmony that was pervasive in the 1960s, but, as with the communal vision of the Living Theater, could not survive the decade's end. What Eden needs most is community, and with the social collapse of the Haight-Ashbury and East Village scenes in an onslaught of hard drugs, external commercial exploitation, and the seemingly endless death-grind of the Vietnam War, an Edenic community proved difficult, if not impossible, to sustain.

Similarly, in Vanderbeek's *Science Friction*, James identifies the film as an example of social critique, a Utopian construct. As he notes,

> In his *Science Friction* . . . the debris from print advertising and the popular press functions simultaneously in two ways. On the

> one hand, it is the major source of imagery by which the satire on the confrontational aspect of the cold war, the arms race, and modern technology in general is articulated; on the other, it is itself the object of satire, the manifestation of a logical connection between the materialistic obsessions of advertising and the permeation of the texture of everyday life by technological overdevelopment. Newspapers themselves turn into missiles, and rockets are constructed out of pictures of the tail fins of fifties automobiles. In one set piece, a TV screen is the frame through which pass two women comparing the brightness of underwear they have washed, a man injecting a brain with a huge hypodermic needle, a Wild West comic, a handgun, a movie cowboy, a collage of brassiere ads, a young woman in a prom dress, and a boxing glove punching out a policeman; a finger switches the set off, but almost immediately the screen is shattered by a rocket. (142–143)

Vanderbeek clearly reveled in the chance to lampoon America's overripe consumer culture, and his inventive collage films offer a refreshing tonic to the inexorable vise of televisual advertisements that marked the late 1950s. Vanderbeek's sound tracks mimic the same manic collagist instinct implicit in his visual constructs; scraps of TV commercial sound tracks, bits of then-contemporary pop music, and segments of the aural portion of TV newscasts compete breathlessly with each other to form a jangling, dissonant vision of a world in psychic overload.

Jack Smith's much-discussed *Flaming Creatures* (1962–1963) offers the dime-store spectacle of a sumptuously costumed transvestite orgy, indebted in equal parts to Maria Montez movies and Smith's own fascination with trash culture. Boasting a truly amazing cast of underground "superstars," all gathered together for this Edenic moment of sexual and sartorial excess, *Flaming Creatures* is at once a parody of Arabian nights excess and also a rapturous explosion of countercultural ecstasy. The numerous participants in the film's production in front of and behind the camera include, as performers, the transgendered Francis Francine and Mario Montez, along with the Living Theater's Judith Malina and composer LaMonte Young's partner, Marian Zazeela. Tony Conrad (who later created the ecstatic filmic vision of light and darkness that is *The Flicker* [1966]) served as the film's sound recordist, while the extras included Conrad, filmmaker Piero Heliczer and his wife Kate, collage artist Ray Johnson, musician Angus MacLise, playwright Ronald Tavel, and numerous other luminaries of the New American Cinema. The film's sound track is comprised of scraps of music from exoticist Hollywood spectacles of the 1930s and '40s, including excerpts from the score for Josef von Sternberg's *The Devil Is a Woman* (1935); Deanna Durbin singing "Amapola" from Henry Koster's *First Love* (1939); portions of the sound track from Arthur Lubin's Technicolor exoticist daydream, *Ali Baba and the Forty Thieves* (1944); and the Everly Brothers singing "Be-Bop-A-Lula" (1958), to name just a few of the many aural source materials (Hoberman 9). The production circumstances of *Flaming Creatures* are threadbare in the extreme. Smith had no money; no one did, and so improvisation was essential to the success of the enterprise.

Smith shot very little film to complete his finished vision of transgendered paradise; indeed, only fifteen minutes of outtakes exist. The film was cut together very rapidly, in less than a week, according to one account, but Tony Conrad's tightly synchronized tape sound track took considerably longer to compile, occupying his time throughout the winter of 1962–1963 (Hoberman 32). After various benefit screenings to raise money to finish the work, the film was screened at the Bleecker Street Cinema on April 29, 1963, with Conrad's tape sound track as accompaniment. The sound track was later converted to a standard 16mm optical track, and the film was printed in a composite version that was distributed through the Film-Makers' Cooperative from 1963 to 1968 (Hoberman 33).

But from its initial screening, *Flaming Creatures* became the object of a vociferous series of legal battles, much too complex to be detailed here. Whether at the Bleecker Street Cinema, the Gramercy Arts Theater, or the Tivoli Theater, screenings of *Flaming Creatures* were routinely the subject of police harassment, and when Jonas Mekas took the film to the Knokke-le-Zout experimental film festival in Belgium, the film was denied a screening on censorship grounds (although Mekas arranged clandestine screenings in his hotel room for the likes of Jean-Luc Godard, Agnes Varda, and Roman Polanski) (Hoberman 40).

Back in the United States, the film was banned nearly everywhere it was shown, and eventually the campaign against the film escalated into a full-fledged court battle, which, starting with an obscenity conviction in the supreme court of New York State, eventually reached the United States Supreme Court, who mooted the verdict in a 5 to 4 decision (Hoberman 47). The film was also screened by Senator Strom Thurmond in the United States Senate office building in an attempt to discredit the Earl Warren Supreme Court (Hoberman 48), but little came of these efforts. Despite campus busts and a continuing public outcry, the film continued to be widely screened.

I remember a 1967 screening at Rutgers University for which I served as the projectionist of the film, where Smith, appearing in person, presented both *Flaming Creatures* and *No President* (1967–1970), in an as-yet-to-be-finalized version; indeed, the film was never really completed. Although everyone present was aware of the film's notoriety, what I remember most is the solicitousness of the campus police who chaperoned the event, surrounding the projector in a circle of chairs to protect Smith and me from any possible disruption by audience members or the local constabulary. I also remember that the print of *Flaming Creatures* was in truly terrible condition, with the sprocket holes torn and double-perforated for the first 100 feet or so of the print, and numerous splices and scratches throughout its entire running time, to the point where the film was almost unprojectable. When I complained to Smith, he mumbled vaguely that I should "do the best" I could, and later complimented me on actually managing to baby the film through the projector. "I usually wind up getting into fistfights with most projectionists," he added. While I was deeply impressed by *Flaming Creatures*, I was more taken with *No President*. The hypnotic lushness of Smith's later film seemed to transport the crowd to a state of quiet, serene contemplation, whereas *Flaming Creatures*, with its famous "Rape-Earthquake-Orgy" (Hoberman 47) sequence, alternately amused and enervated the capacity crowd of more than five hundred. True to form, Smith arrived very late for the screening, without apologies but with film in hand, and when the evening was over, split the box-office take with the Rutgers Film Society in cash and disappeared into the night as mysteriously as he had appeared.

In the final analysis, there was nothing all that shocking about *Flaming Creatures*, even in the 1960s, from the point of view of sexual license. Despite its many supporters, including Susan Sontag, Herman G. Weinberg, producer/director Lewis Allen, filmmakers Shirley Clarke, Willard Van Dyke, and others, the film is still technically classed as obscene "in the boroughs of Manhattan and the Bronx, to this day" (Hoberman 46), but the reason for the fear and distaste that the film inspired has little to do with the sexual activity it contains. Rather, the film constitutes the creation of a homonormative Edenic universe in which that which straight society marginalizes is not only celebrated but also presented as the preferred social mode. As Hoberman concludes in his discussion of the film's legal battles, "As funny as it is poignant, *Flaming Creatures* is guilty of a criminal disrespect more serious than burning the flag. In so casually representing the male organ, it desecrates the underlying symbol of all power structures—including the U.S. Senate" (51). This is the true nature of all Edenic art: to question the nature of the world as it is, and to return it to a state of unexpected innocence. Smith's vision is that of the artist as a social outcast, yet simultaneously as the one who offers early clues to a new direction in gender and social constructs, specifically in the area of human relations. The 1960s were about to explode when Smith made his groundbreaking film; in its own way, *Flaming Creatures* helped to tear down some of the boundaries that existed, by returning women and men to a pansexual garden of Eden.

In this list of Edenic filmmakers of the 1960s, surely one more name should be added, that of Warren Sonbert. Sonbert was arguably the supreme Romantic diarist of the 1960s experimental cinema. His early films are basically diaries: quiet, lyrical records of his friends going through their lives, involved in daily occurrences, shot without preplanning, organization, or logical sequence. The core of Sonbert's early craft is that he created, without complicated camera choreography, editing, or a pronounced story line, films in which one is never conscious of anything but pure emotion. More than any other new American filmmaker of the mid-to-late 1960s, Sonbert creates people who are living and vibrant, reaching out of the screen to enfold the audience in their seductively indolent lives. Sonbert's early cinema is one of intimacies and personal glimpses of the young artists at work in New York. As a filmmaker, Sonbert knew instinctively which moments to film, and his glamorous protagonists thus emerge as genuine personalities existing outside the world of the film.

Born in 1947 in New York City, Warren described his childhood in a 1969 interview with the author as "quiet and uneventful." He had no inclination to make films, and although there was an 8mm camera around the house, he never used it. When he was fifteen, he started going to the Bleecker Street Cinema. One day Sonbert found a large manila envelope on the seat next to him, full of issues of *Film Culture*, *Films in Review*, and other film magazines. He took them home, read them, and began seeing films twelve times a week. Attracted to the work of Howard Hawks and Alfred Hitchcock, Sonbert wrote an angry letter to the manager of the Bleecker Street Cinema, protesting that their work was almost never shown there. Surprisingly, the manager wrote him a letter back, and as the months went by they became good friends. Sonbert got a job as usher at the Bleecker Street, but he spent most of his time meeting filmmakers through the manager. When he was seventeen, Sonbert met filmmaker Gregory Markopolous, who loaned him his Bolex camera and encouraged him to make films. Although he shot a couple of 100-foot rolls of 16mm film, Sonbert was still reluctant to begin filmmaking, feeling himself inadequately tutored.

To rectify this, upon graduation from high school Sonbert enrolled at New York University to study film. In his second year at NYU, Sonbert made his first 16mm movie, *Amphetamine,* an early gay-themed film centering around the lives of two friends of Sonbert's who shared a predilection for injecting speed. The film was screened publicly at the Bleecker Street Cinema for a number of critics and filmmakers who were enthusiastic in their praise of the film, and Sonbert's career was truly launched. The film was shot over a weekend in February 1966 at Sonbert's apartment with borrowed equipment and outdated black-and-white film stock; it begins with shots of several young men shooting up amphetamine, talking, laughing, and drinking soda. This is followed by a long shot of rippling light (actually footage from an aborted documentary on the denizens of Forty-second Street in New York; the film had gotten jammed in the camera during shooting and was considered unusable, until Sonbert realized that it could be employed as a segue for this later film), and then a shock cut to two boys passionately kissing, as the camera swoops ecstatically around them.

Amphetamine was followed by *Where Did Our Love Go?* (shot in June 1966), a fifteen-minute color film with a taped sound track, documenting Sonbert's friends going to movies, eating, and shopping for clothes. James Stoller described the film as "both a valentine and a farewell to a generation, as well as being simply a portrait which is tender, distant, accurate, somewhat high, and sad. . . . I could watch this film a hundred times; it made me feel old, older than I am, but also it opened my eyes and my heart" (FMC 141). Next was *Hall of Mirrors* (shot in October 1966), a seven-minute film shot in color and black-

and-white. The film opens with, in Sonbert's words, "Fredric March and Florence Eldridge lost in a 1948 hall of mirrors" (actually re-edited outtakes from Michael Gordon's film *An Act of Murder*), and then segues into a one-reel sequence of poet/artist René Ricard crying in a dimly lit apartment. The final sequence shows Gerard Malanga walking through a mirror sculpture in a New York art gallery. The sound track consists of two pop songs, "What Becomes of the Broken Hearted?" and "Walk Away Renee" and ends with a section of Georges Delerue's score for Jean-Luc Godard's film *Contempt* (1963). It was also during this time that Sonbert shot many of the key scenes for Gerard Malanga's *In Search of the Miraculous,* in particular the film's opening sequence of Malanga pirouetting on the tiled walk in front of the Columbia University Library.

From this point on, Sonbert abandoned any pretense at narrative and began to carry the camera with him as he went about, shooting whatever seemed to him to be worth recording. Except for *Hall of Mirrors,* all of Sonbert's early films are presented as a succession of largely unedited reels, straight from the camera, presented with a backdrop of pop music. In this style he made *The Tenth Legion* (1966), *Truth Serum* (shot in April 1967), *The Bad and the Beautiful* (shot in October 1967), and *Holiday* (shot in February 1968). Sonbert had several highly successful shows of these films at the Cinematheque, as well as screenings at the Jewish Museum and the Elgin Theater.

With the help of a generous graduation gift of money from his mother, Warren left the country for Morocco in April of 1969. Before leaving he withdrew almost all of his work from distribution. It was re-released in the early 1970s. For the rest of his life Warren kept his film diary and presented various versions of footage old and new in a series of revised, silent films, including *Carriage Trade* (1968–1972), *Rude Awakening* (1972–1976), *Divided Loyalties* (1975–1978), *Noblesse Oblige* (1978–1981), *A Woman's Touch* (1981–1983), *The Cup and the Lip* (1986), *Honor and Obey* (1988), and several other works, films that often used extensive sections from Sonbert's earlier works. As is well known, Sonbert never used work prints for his films. Since all of his

15. Gerard Malanga in his deeply romantic portrait of the artist in love, *In Search of the Miraculous* (1967). Photograph courtesy of Anthology Film Archives.

material was shot on color reversal film, he would project the materials, make notes, and then edit and re-edit the footage until he was satisfied with the result.

But Sonbert was never really satisfied with his work and kept editing his films for the rest of his life, which sadly ended much too prematurely. Sonbert ultimately died of complications due to AIDS on May 31, 1995, leaving behind a body of gorgeously evocative work that indelibly recalls Manhattan in the 1960s, a period of youth, ambition, and innocence, where time seemed to stand still. There was always another party to go to, and living was both easy and inexpensive. In many ways Sonbert's work is the ultimate witness to the Edenic era of pre-AIDS sexuality. When the times changed, Warren changed with them, but as someone who knew him well during the final years of the 1960s, I feel that he was most content in the early part of his career, when life was an adventure, and an informal but vital network of friendships and shared intimacies bound us all together as one. In his article "Saint Warren," David Ehrenstein had this to say of Sonbert's early, and, some would argue, most evocative and personal work:

> that which is most appealing in Warren Sonbert's films has little to do with "subject" or "technique," but rather concerns certain aspects of Sonbert's personality as expressed through his films—specifically his goodness. Warren Sonbert possesses a sensibility both of its time and outside it. Of it for its manifestations of contemporary preoccupations (drugs, clothes, sex, etc.), and outside it because of Sonbert's purity of documentation, innocence of regard—saintliness. . . . To quote Lorenzo Mans, "It would be nice if life were like a Warren Sonbert movie." (19)

The intensity and honesty of Sonbert's Edenic cinema is emblematic of most of the work produced by the 1960s avant-garde, whether in Manhattan or San Francisco, as well as the work of the performance artists of the era, who also contributed their own vision of a society without walls. The Japanese artist Kazuo Shiraga's *Challenging Mud*

(1955) was an early performance piece, or "action," in which the artist, sprawled in a pool of mud, attempted to navigate from one edge of the pool to the other (Schimmel 25). Saburó Murakami's *Breaking Through Many Screens of Paper* (1956) was another early "action" piece, in which the artist plunged through a series of upright paper canvases, as if breaking through to a new consciousness, as indeed he was, liberated from the traditional definition of what constituted art (Schimmel 27). Atsuko Tanaka created one of the most spectacular performance costumes of the era with her *Electric Dress* (1956), a body covering composed almost entirely of incandescent and fluorescent lightbulbs in a wide array of colors, which transformed the artist's body into a whirling vortex of light and motion (Schimmel 28).

The French artist Yves Klein popularized the use of "living paintbrushes," in which he covered nude models with paint (Klein's favorite color was a shocking ultramarine blue) and then had them roll around on large canvases placed on the floor. Klein called this process "anthropometry" and created a large number of pieces in the late 1950s and early 1960s celebrating the connection of the human body to the direct act of creation. Questioned as to his guiding philosophy, Klein replied, "Art, it is health! This health makes us exist. [It is] all that we are" (qtd. in Schimmel 35). Guiseppe Pinot Gallizio created his installation *The Cave of Antimatter* (*La Caverna dell'antimateria*) in Torino, Italy, in 1959, composed entirely of the artist's "industrial paintings" (works created using "fast-drying resins, spray guns, and long rolls of canvas"), and declared that it represented the "uterus of the world" (Schimmel 49). In the aftermath of the new atomic age, Gallizio argued, it was up to artists to reclaim the humanity of the arts.

Allan Kaprow became famous for his series of "happenings," beginning in 1958, in which painting, sculpture, cinema, and performance were combined to create an Edenic vision of earthly paradise, a world transformed by the power of art (Schimmel 58–63). In Russia the conceptual artists Valery Gerlovina and Rimma Gerlovina performed *Zoo* (1976), in which the artists sat nude behind bars in a prison cell, while a sign outside the cage proclaimed "Homosapiens Male and Female," in a direct gesture of protest against the exploitation of artists, humans, and animals within contemporary society (Klocker 167). Valie Export's famous *Touch and Taste Film (Tapp und tastkino)*, executed in 1968 with the participation of fellow artist Peter Weibel, challenged audience members to physically experience the female human body as a part of an Edenic performance piece, as "Export appeared on the street with a miniature theater-stage set constructed around her bare, but hidden, breasts. Using a bullhorn, Weibel invited the public to step up, reach through the stage curtains, and touch her breasts" (Stiles 266).

Filmmaker/performance artist Carolee Schneemann, famous for her landmark film *Fuses* (1964–1967), a gorgeously sensuous love poem in which the artist and her partner James Tenney make love, rendered all the more transcendent through the artist's carefully considered use of different film stocks, color filters, and seemingly extradiegetic material (Schneemann's cat looking out the window as the wind blows through the curtains), also created a series of performance pieces in which she used her body as a medium of human agency and social commentary. This work was a continuation of her own activity as a performance artist in such pieces as *Meat Joy* (1964), which Schneemann described as a "propulsion . . . toward the ecstatic—shifting and turning between tenderness, wildness, precision, abandon: qualities which could at any moment be sensual, comic, joyous, repellent, [and] an erotic rite: excessive, indulgent, a celebration of [male and female] flesh as material" (qtd. in Stiles 270).

Shigeko Kubota's *Vagina Painting*, performed on July 4, 1965, linked the female body's menstrual cycle with the act of creation as Kubota painted on a piece of paper on the floor with a brush dipped in red paint, which she had fastened to her undergarments (Stiles 279). In Paul Neagu's *Going Tornado* (1975),

> the artist became a whirling dervish spinning like a gyroscope. Attached to his spinning body, he fastened cultural baggage (his rolled-up clothing) which he used as a kind of "ballast" to enable

> him to spin faster. As [Neagu] wrote, "The quasi-ecstatic character of a 'tornado' as culminative within the cycle is its expurgative and absorptive flow, that is to say it is an extravagant and wasteful disentanglement transcending everything which enters its whirls." (Stiles 327)

This attempt to extend the consciousness of the human body, to transcend the physical and achieve a melding of the spiritual and corporeal worlds, is the ultimate ambition of all Edenic performance art. It is an effort to break free of the constraints of the body, of sexual identification and physical limitations, to extend the boundaries of that which is human into the territory of the unknown, to achieve a state of spiritual ecstasy in which all the senses are deranged, or perhaps more accurately, rearranged, and reconfigured to produce a new series of sensations and responses to the central fact of one's humanity.

As Jonas Mekas wrote when the first intermedia shows began to appear as public performance pieces in the mid 1960s,

> Suddenly, the intermedia shows are all over the town. . . . The [Exploding] Plastic Inevitables' (Velvet Underground; Warhol and Company) performances at the Dom during the month of April provided the loudest and most dynamic exploration platform for this new art. . . . At the other, almost opposite, end is the USCO show (at the Riverside Museum)—the show that sums up everything that USCO has done till now. . . . [It] is a search for religious, mystical experience. Whereas in the case of Plastic Inevitables the desire for the mystical experience is unconscious, the USCO is going after it in a more conscious way. They have arrived somewhere, and gained a certain peace, certain insights, and now they are beginning to meditate. (243)

Though the Edenic spirit of the 1960s has passed into memory, the numerous filmic records of the happenings and light shows of the era (as in Ron Nameth's *Andy Warhol's E.P.I.* [1968], which captures the Exploding Plastic Inevitables' performances at the peak of their power, or Raymond Saroff's invaluable and pastoral records of Claes Oldenburg's 1962 "Happenings," staged in a storefront on East Second Street in Manhattan in *Store Days I and II*, *Necropolis I and II*, *World's Fair II*, *Voyages II*, and *Happenings I and II* [all 1962]), exist to remind us of this fertile period in American art, which still, despite all of society's troubles, continues to inspire a new generation of artists.

Foremost among the Edenicists of today is perhaps the Swiss video installation artist Pipilotti Rist, whose warm, humane, and gently humorous works include *Mistakes* (1988) and *Ever Is All Over* (1997), possibly her most famous piece. In this work the artist strolls down a street in a Zurich suburb wielding a huge metal flower, which she uses to ritualistically smash car windows as she passes by, unimpeded by a policewoman who smiles and nods as Rist walks along. This loop image is coupled with a complementary video that displays glorious flowers in full bloom, as if to foreground the regenerative power of nature. In *Ever Is All Over*, violence against the mechanized world is seen as cathartic, and Rist notes that "I passionately believe that we can achieve human and cultural progress only through pieces of work that are formulated in positive terms. I can undermine entrenched ideas better by creating images based on, say, a moment of joy in the midst of embarrassment, or love inspired by bizarre details" (Rist 1999).

Rist's newest work, *Saffron Flower or Fall Time Less (Herbstzeitlose)*, which premiered at the Luhring Augustine Gallery in New York on September 11, 2004—a date that, for all New Yorkers, is inextricably intertwined with the tragic events of the World Trade Center disaster three years earlier—offers a much-needed counterbalance to the solemn remembrance of that day and continues the artist's preoccupations with the heavenly in the everyday life, as she weaves a sinuous tapestry of light and shadow using common household objects—spatulas, ice-cube trays, forks, spoons—hung in the gallery space by string, casting shadows on the walls where a video image of the bucolic Swiss countryside is projected, seemingly unchanging, but in fact constantly transmuted by time, light, shadow, and clouds.

Rist describes the installation as an "interweaving of inside and outside, subjectivity and environment" (Rist 2004), which strikes a deeply personal note for both the artist and the viewer. The images projected on the wall were photographed in the Swiss countryside near Rist's childhood home in Gallen, Switzerland; as the viewer enters the gallery space, Rist has provided a bench and the back porch of "a typical Swiss country home" (Rist 2004), where the viewer may sit and contemplate the spectacle before her/him. If the viewer prefers, s/he may move around the exhibit and interact with the installation by gently touching the suspended kitchen objects, so that they create new shadowed patterns on the walls of the video piece.

Saffron Flower or Fall Time Less (Herbstzeitlose) was premiered with another new work by Rist, *Tombstone for RW (Grabstein für RW)*, which functions as a video memorial for an artist friend who has passed from this world to the next. As Rist notes, "the work invokes a dialogue between mortal and spiritual, [and . . .] confronts the notion of passing on from this life, and commemorates it joyously" (Rist 2004). The images in this second piece are less specific and center almost solely on light as the source and content of the work, suggesting that we are born into the light and then return to it.

Rist's work is in stark contrast to the negativism of much video art in the twentieth century, which suggests limits rather than transcendence; she invites the viewer to participate directly in the work as a performer and an observer simultaneously. The marked difference between either of these works and what passes for entertainment in contemporary video games is striking; Rist is seeking to compose a positive, joyous universe that all may enter, rather than indulging in exclusionary, elitist tactics, or confrontational work that forces the viewer to submit to the spectacle s/he witnesses. In many ways, Rist's optimism is a throwback to the Edenic spirit of the 1960s; perhaps, one hopes, it prefigures an early clue to a new and more life-affirming direction in contemporary art.

The archetypal West Coast Edenic Beat film, *The Flower Thief* (1960), directed by Ron Rice, exemplifies this rejection of conventional values in every aspect of its production. Shot on a nonexistent budget, using severely outdated 50-foot cartridges of World War II surplus gunnery film as raw stock, *The Flower Thief* follows actor-performer Taylor Mead, the Charlie Chaplin of the 1960s underground, on a series of picaresque adventures in and around San Francisco. The film has little plot and needs none; the title of the film derives from a random incident in which Mead steals a flower from a street vendor and then fantasizes that the police are about to arrest him for his crime. Escaping down the steep San Francisco streets in a Radio Flyer—a child's wagon—desperately clutching his much-abused teddy bear, Mead is at once pathetic and endearing, projecting an image of holy foolishness on the screen. As the film progresses through its seventy-five-minute running time, Mead interacts with groups of roving beatniks, schoolchildren, jazz musicians, and North Beach hustlers to create a portrait of a man unfettered by the constraints of society. The sound track is an asynchronous mélange of Beat poetry, jazz music, and Serge Prokofiev's *Peter and the Wolf*, recorded on a reel-to-reel tape machine. Considered perhaps the most uncompromising and genuinely avant-garde feature film of the early 1960s, *The Flower Thief* is a paean to the plight of the outsider in a world that is both unresponsive and unyielding.

When Ron Rice planned to shoot *The Flower Thief*, he had no money, only a vague idea and the services of Taylor Mead as his lead actor. Using a primitive 16mm camera and a fierce tenacity of spirit, Rice impulsively wrote letters to numerous major Hollywood producers asking for support for his totally anarchic, completely scriptless and plotless film. Combining threats with blandishments, Rice's letters proved spectacularly ineffective, until perhaps the least likely of all possible sponsors, "B" film producer Sam Katzman, donated "five thousand feet of unused 16mm war surplus machine gun film [to record aerial bomber strikes] for [Rice's] vision" (Rice 117).

The film immediately commenced production with only the barest possible raw materials, and yet it eventually surfaced in New York as a substantive commercial success; a feature film literally made out of

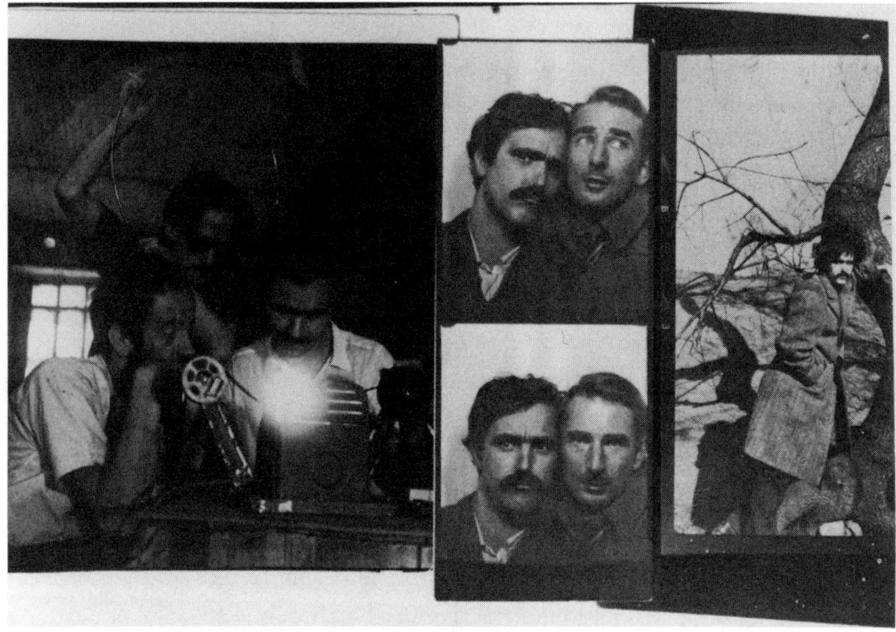

16. In love with the cinema: a. Taylor Mead, left, seated, with Ron Rice, seated, edit *Queen of Sheba Meets the Atom Man* (1963), as filmmaker Jerry Joffen stands in the background; b. Ron Rice, left, and filmmaker Jack Smith in a photo booth session in Times Square; c. Ron Rice poses next to a tree in the late 1950s. Photograph courtesy of Anthology Film Archives.

nothing more than ambition, faith, and an Edenic vision of earthly paradise (see Hoberman 97 for more on the film's near rapturous critical reception). Rice, an extravagantly and deeply individualistic talent, was possessed of a vision that could break down all the barriers placed in front of him except that of his own mortality. Exhausted, working too hard, and without money, Rice died in Acapulco, Mexico, in December of 1964 and was buried there on Christmas Day (Mekas 171). But his visionary spirit lives on in his notebooks and diaries, which are filled with plans for numerous ambitious projects, several of which he was able to realize on earth. In addition to *The Flower Thief*, Rice also completed the films *Senseless* (1962), *Chumlum* (1964), the unfinished feature *Queen of Sheba Meets the Atom Man* (1963), and several rolls of footage shot in Mexico just before his death. But as great as his accomplishment was, Rice's death cut short his earthly tenure as an artist. The balance of his work, as Mekas wrote in Rice's obituary on December 31, 1964, would have to be created in Heaven (Mekas 170–172).

CHAPTER FOUR

The Uses of Heaven

Since the cinema is inherently a zone of fantasy, a place where the self can be projected at will in whatever guise one wishes, it is an ideal location for visions of the next world, whether paradisiacal or not. Cinema aspires to complete the work of imagined constructs of Heaven by giving imagistic solidity to that which must be taken on faith; we will never know whether or not Heaven exists until we die, and then we will be beyond the reach of those who would wish to communicate with us. The cinema itself represents a kind of quotidian Heaven, in which the daily concerns of existence can be put to one side for a moment, and the viewer can forget his or her cares for a few hours before returning to the world of the actual. The film palaces of the 1920s and 1930s stressed this air of unreality in their over-the-top grandeur; this was not the real world, but rather the world of "stars" in the cinematic firmament. For all of us, life is a continual balancing act in which we bargain for security and safety by buying a house, paying insurance, holding a job, and believing in our work as if that work itself represented our actual world. But it does not; our bodies, which are by definition mortal, encompass our world. The boundary between the self and the image on the screen is inviolate; one can only regard the images of paradise that the cinema offers us with a sense of wonder and dismay that the world we must inhabit is such a consistently dangerous place, a zone of continual risk and uncertainty. The cinema allows us to become disembodied for a short space of time and forces our visual and aural consciousness to the forefront, while we remain immobile in our seats, watching.

The cinema offers us a vision of the world as we would have it, rather than as it is; horror films provide a dystopian vision of "risk" without genuine danger; projections of Heaven afford us the assurance that this life is simply an intermediate point on our journey, and that when we die, we will join those we love and live a life free from want and uncertainty. The work of Heaven in the cinema, then, is to give us reassurance and guidance, as the medium of the cinematograph allows those who have departed to instruct and entertain us anew, restored to life through the trope of the moving image. In M. Night Shyamalan's *The Sixth Sense* (1999), Cole Sear (Haley Joel Osment) complains insistently, "I see dead people." But we all do, whenever we go to the movies or watch a film from the 1940s that restores the past to us anew. The dead and the living intermingle quite comfortably within the world of the cinema, and so it is fitting that, in Hollywood's visions of the next world, the hand of divine providence should so often reach out to give the living a bit of much needed assistance.

One of the most unusual examples of celestial intervention in the cinema is undoubtedly Gregory La Cava's *Gabriel Over the White House* (1933), in which Walter Huston plays political hack Judson Hammond, who is elected to the office of president of the United States with the expectation that he will be a caretaker president, interested only in the problems of the wealthy. At first his backers' faith seems justified: Hammond makes vague speeches about helping to end the Depression, offers a few political plans to his closest associates, and spends most of his time at parties or partisan political functions. But one day, speeding in the presidential motorcade as a lark to annoy his detail of Secret Service agents, President Hammond plunges off a bend in the road, through a picket fence, and down a steep ravine, sustaining serious injuries. The White House physician, Dr. Eastman (Samuel S. Hinds), holds out little hope for recovery as the president sinks deeper into a coma. But just when it seems that all is lost, a vision of

17. Walter Huston, as the divinely inspired president Judson Hammond, speaks to the nation in Gregory La Cava's *Gabriel Over the White House* (1933). Photograph courtesy of The Jerry Ohlinger Archives.

the Archangel Gabriel mysteriously appears to the president in a haze of blinding light, wordlessly instructing Hammond as to how to handle the affairs of the nation.

While the members of his cabinet fret over their futures, Hammond regains consciousness but admonishes Dr. Eastman that no one must know of his recovery, at least not yet—Hammond needs time to make his plans for a new nation. When he emerges from his bedchamber, Hammond is transformed; his geniality and ease of manner have been replaced by a stern countenance and an unshakable determination to take the affairs of the country in hand. Enlisting the aid of his trusted assistant, Hartley Beekman (Franchot Tone), Hammond abruptly fires his cabinet, revokes the Constitution, declares martial law, and sidesteps impeachment proceedings by dissolving the power of the Congress, declaring himself the absolute dictator of the nation. All of these acts he accomplishes through the power of his will alone; his manner, once approachable, becomes that of a visionary patriarch who will brook no dissent from his followers. Meeting with John Bronson (David Landau), the leader of an army of jobless men who have marched to the Capitol in search of aid, Hammond boldly walks out of the White House and addresses Bronson and the homeless veterans in a public square, promising them jobs as part of a national recovery project (similar in style to FDR's NRA), for which they will be paid "army wages."

Hammond also outlines plans for a financial safety net for those who are unable to work (FDR's Social Security plan), winning over the hostile crowd in a matter of minutes and paving the way to a new socialist nation. With these programs under way, Hammond turns his attention to "the evils of the Eighteenth Amendment," ordering an immediate end to Prohibition (as FDR did) as an aid to national recovery. Not surprisingly, elements of organized crime take a dim view of this last development, and when Bronson and his army of now gainfully employed men back the president, the leader of the crime bosses, Nick Diamond (C. Henry Gordon), has Bronson brutally murdered. In a blind rage, President Hammond calls out his new brigade of brownshirts to storm the gangster's fortress-like citadel and, using tanks and heavy weaponry, forces the crooks to surrender. Within hours Diamond and his associates are lined up before a firing squad, without benefit of even a military trial, and summarily executed. Beekman, the president's aide, presides over the mass execution with a grim smile of satisfaction, wearing the new uniform of Hammond's brownshirts as their de facto commander in chief, whose only loyalty is to President Hammond.

With the country now on an economic rebound, Hammond turns his thoughts to international affairs, again guided by visions of the angel Gabriel, who appears periodically throughout the film in a flood of celestial light that illuminates the president's face with heavenly radiance. Convinced that the only way to restore the nation's place in the world is to immediately collect on all debts owed to the U.S. by foreign nations, Hammond stages a demonstration for the leaders of the key European nations on a battleship and promises to destroy the other nations of the world with "weapons of mass destruction too terrible to contemplate," including "death rays and powerful new bombs." To drive home his point Hammond has American planes sink a mothballed battleship as a demonstration of American air superiority in front of the astonished heads of state and their diplomatic staff. The choice, Hammond declares, is simple: "Repay the loans we have made to you in your time of need, or face annihilation from the air."

Not surprisingly, France, England, and the other allies immediately agree and assemble at the White House to sign a unilateral peace treaty, which forces all the nations of the world to disarm except for the United States, which will serve as peacekeeper to the world. As the leaders of the free world sign the document one by one, President Hammond looks on with weary determination. When it becomes time for him to affix his signature to the document, he takes out a fountain pen and then pauses and decides to use a quill pen instead, as a gesture signifying the start of the New American Revolution, evoking memories of the United States' initial break with Britain nearly 150 years earlier. Just as Hammond laboriously completes signing the pact, he is felled by a stroke. This time he will not regain consciousness; within minutes, President Hammond is dead.

This astonishing film has a deeply curious provenance. Shot in less than two weeks (February 16 to 25, 1932) for $180,000 (Bernstein 83), the film was financed by none other than press baron William Randolph Hearst through his Cosmopolitan Pictures Corporation, which served primarily as a vehicle for producing a string of unsuccessful musical comedies starring Marion Davies (Hearst's mistress) and other light fare. Through a blanket agreement with MGM, all Cosmopolitan productions were distributed through MGM, which was then operating under the equally dictatorial control of Louis B.

Mayer. Mayer, a diehard Republican, was appalled by the production and shelved it for several months, fearing that it would reflect badly on the Hoover administration, then in power in Washington. Hearst, at the time an avid supporter of Roosevelt's proposals for an "activist presidency" (which he would later bitterly regret), became intimately involved in the film, dictating portions of the script and even the text of some of President Hammond's speeches (Bernstein 84).

Things became still more complex when the Hays Office (the motion picture industry's censorship authority) intervened, claiming that the film would foster notions of "revolution" and present the United States government in an unfavorable light abroad (Bernstein 85). When the film was previewed in Glendale in March of 1933, Mayer was aghast, and ordered associate producer Eddie Mannix to "put that picture back in its can, take it back to the studio, and lock it up!" (Bernstein 86). Only after a good deal of editing, and some more retakes, was the film finally released on March 29, 1933; it was a modest box-office success and aroused a certain amount of controversy in the press (Bernstein 86).

Mayer fervently believed that Hoover would be reelected, but public sentiment against the incumbent was overwhelming, and Roosevelt was swept to power in the 1932 election. Mayer was then more than happy to release the film as widely as possible, to suggest to the public that Roosevelt would prove a dangerous and unscrupulous dictator as president. When FDR did, in fact, institute a number of the measures outlined in *Gabriel Over the White House* (the abolition of Prohibition, the enactment of Social Security, and the forty-hour work week, as well as the NRA, the WPA, and other social recovery programs), Mayer was delighted. Surely Roosevelt would now be exposed for the power-mad tyrant that he was.

But Mayer reckoned before the rise of the Axis powers (whom Hearst initially admired for their "law and order" approach to public government), which made fascism suddenly unfashionable, and the country's subsequent involvement in World War II after years of isolationism. FDR stayed in power until 1945, serving an unprecedented three terms in office and elected to a fourth, before his death from a cerebral hemorrhage in Warm Springs, Georgia, cut his tenure as chief executive short. In his attempt to pack the Supreme Court when the National Recovery Administration was ruled unconstitutional, FDR did indeed display a flair for Machiavellian manipulation. But unlike the fictional Hammond, when public opinion solidified against FDR's proposed alteration of the court, the president relented (*American Experience*).

If heavenly intervention in politics is one of the uses to which Heaven can be enlisted, Alice Guy's *The Birth, Life, and Death of Our Lord Jesus Christ* (*La naissance, la vie, et la mort de Notre-Seigneur Jésus-Christ*, 1906), better known as *The Life of Christ* (*La vie du Christ*), in which she used the flamboyant Victorin-Hippolyte Jasset (who is often erroneously credited with direction of the film) as her production designer, envisions Christ's life, teachings, death, and resurrection as a feminist parable, existing in a world in which women and children dominate each of the film's twenty-five tableaux. Guy, born in 1875, began her career working as secretary to Léon Gaumont, the pioneering French producer/distributor, and on her lunch breaks, began to make short films to demonstrate Gaumont's early motion picture cameras. *The Cabbage Patch Fairy* (*La fée aux choux*, 1896), shot several months before Georges Méliès began producing his films, gave Guy the title of the world's first director of a narrative film.

In *The Cabbage Patch Fairy*, a maternal fairy finds young babies in the cabbage patch for expectant young mothers (in much the same way that the stork is a symbol of childbirth in American folklore); the finished film runs approximately one minute in length. By 1906 she had directed 181 short films for Gaumont, including early experiments in synchronized sound recording (using a wax cylinder machine), which Gaumont dubbed the "Chronophone," and color hand and machine tinting, to add additional visual flair to her work (see McMahan 43–77 for a discussion of Guy's use of sound and color in her early films).

The Life of Christ envisions a world in which Christ is a benevolent agent of social change, attended to by women and children as his pri-

18. Angels attend the sleeping baby Jesus in Alice Guy's *The Birth, Life, and Death of Our Lord Jesus Christ* (1906). Photograph courtesy of The Jerry Ohlinger Archives.

mary constituents. The men in the film are, for the most part, Christ's tormentors and detractors, or the Roman soldiers who crucify Him, or members of the Apostles. There are men present in Guy's luxurious mise-en-scène, to be sure, but the frame is dominated by women as his most fervent adherents, his most sympathetic followers, and his most faithful servants. With sumptuous sets designed by Henri Ménessier, *The Life of Christ* is at once an embrace of all humanity, as well as a celebration of general differentiation and of Guy's own career as a woman filmmaker in an industry largely dominated by men.

Always the visionary, in 1906 she directed the groundbreaking Gaumont production *The Results of Feminism* (*Les résultats du féminisme*), a social critique in which (according to the film's press book) "men [are] reduced to doing their own washing, ironing, sewing, and even making hats for their wives" (qtd. in McMahan 235). In 1907 she married producer/director Herbert Blaché. In 1912, as her own producer at Solax, the American production company she had founded in 1910, she remade the film as *In the Year 2000*, depicting a future era in which "women shall rule the Earth . . . and men shall be subordinates and adjuncts" (qtd. in McMahan 234).

Unfortunately, as with most of Alice Guy Blaché's work, both films are lost; indeed, of her total output of (at best estimate) 244 films as director, only 111 films survive; the other films became the victims of nitrate decomposition, poor preservation, and the sexism of conventional film historians, who failed to significantly value Guy Blaché's work in the shadow of her more aggressively self-promotional contemporaries, particularly D. W. Griffith. It should be noted that of the 111 surviving films, many of these are still awaiting preservation, and only a handful of her shorts—perhaps a dozen in all—are generally available to the public. The rest reside in archives, awaiting the funding that would restore them to the public at large.

With the eventual collapse of Solax, Guy Blaché found work as a "director for hire," with no thematic or artistic control over the films she directed from 1914 onward; she made her last film in 1920 and divorced in 1922 (McMahan 173). While it would be easy to misread her later life as a tragic period of abandonment, we should remember that her accomplishments as a director—the 111 films that survive, and the others that have attained a phantom existence of sorts through surviving scripts, still photographs, and promotional materials—present us with an Edenic world of social and sexual equality, in which women and men work in harmony, and life has become a domestic paradise on Earth. Many of Guy Blaché's films deal with interrupted love affairs that are "put right" through the intervention of the woman involved in the troubled romance; in *The Girl in the Armchair* (1913), one of her Solax shorts that still survives, a resourceful woman covers up her fiancé's theft of her father's money that he purloined to cover his gambling debts, at which point the young man confesses all to her fa-

19. The crucifixion of Jesus in Alice Guy's *The Birth, Life, and Death of Our Lord Jesus Christ* (1906). Photograph courtesy of The Jerry Ohlinger Archives.

ther, and is forgiven. In *Matrimony's Speed Limit* (1913), another surviving film, a young woman grows tired of waiting for her beloved to propose and tricks him into marriage with a faked telegram, stating that he must marry immediately in order to inherit an enormous fortune; the young man marries her after a series of comic misadventures.

In *His Double* (1912), a young woman is told by her father to marry a man she does not care for. Disguising her true love as the would-be suitor, she deceives her father and the clergyman who marries them; faced with his daughter's persistence, her father accepts the "trick" marriage. *A House Divided* (1913) depicts a married couple engaged in such a bitter quarrel that they agree to communicate only through written notes; by the film's end, they realize the absurdity of their estrangement and break the spell with a kiss. For Guy Blaché, her perpetual dream was the heterotopic paradise of a union of the sexes as working, equal partners, as seen in one of her final films as a director, *When You and I Were Young* (1917). In the film, as McMahan so poignantly relates, "a young man and a young woman marry and both pursue their chosen artistic careers, though at first this gets them disowned by their respective families. The families come around eventually however; Guy's message here, as always, is to be true to oneself and everything else will work out" (241). In the feminist and deeply romantic world of Alice Guy Blaché's cinema, there is always a solution to the problems of everyday existence, and life, as inspired by the example of Heaven (she was a devout Catholic), will always be a potentially Edenic locale.

More conventionally patriarchal visions of Heaven in the cinema are, of course, numerous; if we are unhappy or ill-treated in this world, the dominant cinema reminds us, we will probably be rewarded with an unceasing paradise in the next. In Harold S. Bucquet's *On Borrowed Time* (1939), Julian Northrup (Lionel Barrymore), confined to a wheelchair (in real life, as in the film), refuses to accompany death, in the form of Mr. Brink (Sir Cedric Hardwicke), to Heaven when his time has come. Through a series of machinations, Julian traps Mr. Brink in an apple tree in his backyard and renders him powerless. In the absence of death, *On Borrowed Time* persuasively argues, those for whom death would serve as a release have their lives artificially extended, only to exist in a world of pain and suffering.

In a rather cruel scene, it is not until Dr. Brink convinces Julian's grandson, John "Pud" Northrup (Bobs Watson), to climb the tree for an apple—thus precipitating what should be a fatal fall for the youngster—that Julian relents. Deprived of the solace of death, Pud lingers in agony until Julian, unable to bear the thought of Pud's continual suffering, frees Mr. Brink from the tree. In the film's final, deeply moving scene, Julian's ability to walk is restored (through the aid of rear-screen projection) as he and Pud accompany Mr. Brink to Heaven and remark that they never knew how "beautiful it would be, how free of pain."

Nodding knowingly, Mr. Brink quietly admonishes them, "I told you that it would be best to come with me," and the film ends with the balance of life and death restored at last. The film's implicit message is clear: to have life, there must be death—which, however, is viewed through the theist lens of Christian mythology as the precursor to eternal life. If Heaven assuredly awaits us, who would not be eager to die?

In many Hollywood fantasies about Heaven, the dead return to assist the living as an angelic presence, usually invisible to the world at large. In Victor Fleming's macho fantasy *A Guy Named Joe* (1943), bomber pilot Major Pete Sandidge (Spencer Tracy) is killed in action during World War II (due in part, it is implied, to his daredevil tactics in combat). Under the guidance of another deceased pilot, Captain Dick Rumney (Barry Nelson), who is now an angel, and the supervisor of the General (Lionel Barrymore as a deceased but unnamed World War I air "ace," whose imposing angelic presence dominates the film as a whole), Sandidge is sent back to Earth to train and inspire a new generation of fighter pilots, in particular Captain Ted Randall (Van Johnson), who has fallen in love with Sandidge's old flame, Dorinda Durston (Irene Dunne). Though indignant at first when given his assignment, Sandidge soon realizes the value of his earthly mission (after all, it is pointed out to him repeatedly—"Who do you think helped you out when you were in training?"—implying that angelic presences in everyday life are a constant factor in the success of one's daily affairs).

A Guy Named Joe is primarily a wartime recruiting tool, which assures young recruits that they are fighting on God's side and that with the assistance of Divine intervention their victory in battle is assured. Naturally, the Japanese fliers in World War II also believed, and were taught to believe by Japanese war films, radio, and print media, that they were equally favored by the gods, culminating in the appalling spectacle of the Kamikaze (the "Divine Wind"; see Inoguchi) pilots crashing their aircraft into Allied battleships in a suicidal bid to save the Empire from destruction as well as guarantee themselves a place in paradise (Miller and Commager 419–420). But for American fighter pilots, even though many war films gave token attention to alternative faiths, the predominant cultural focus was on a Christian theocracy where those who fought on "our side" were assured of eternal life, especially if they died while in the performance of their duties. Although the message was presented in a more subtle and enticing fashion, films such as *A Guy Named Joe* made death attractive through the promise of a life eternal after death, a life where we may, in fact, rejoin and influence the living.

Michael Powell and Emeric Pressburger's epic fantasy *A Matter of Life and Death* (British, 1946) is known in the United States under the more prosaic but perhaps more accurate title *Stairway to Heaven,* since much of the film's action takes place on a giant staircase ascending into paradise. Fighter pilot Peter Carter (David Niven) is shot down in combat and uses his last moments in the air to contact American-born RAF radio operator June (Kim Hunter), telling her of his approximate location, and, improbably (yet in keeping with the traditions of the wartime romance film, in which life is always mediated by the prospect of death, so that every second becomes ineffably precious), falling in love with her as his plane plunges toward Earth. Bailing out at the last minute, Peter regains consciousness at the edge of the ocean.

But, as one might expect, there has been a flaw in the system; Peter was not destined to survive the destruction of his aircraft, but Conductor 71 (Marius Goring), who was to guide him to Heaven, has forgotten to collect him, "missing him in all that fog." Arguing that matters have changed since the hour of his appointed "death" because of his love for June, Peter appeals to Heaven for a tribunal, arguing that because of the conductor's error he now has the right to live. The appeal is granted, much to the delight of Peter and his deceased and thus now-angelic former flying partner Bob Trapshaw (Robert Coote). There is, however, another problem. The prosecution is put in the hands of Abraham Farlan (Raymond Massey), an American patriot from Boston, who was fatally wounded by a British bullet during the Revolutionary War, and hates all things English. In the meantime, the still-living-but-under-sentence-of-death Peter is diagnosed by Dr. Reeves (Roger Livesey) as being the victim of hallucinations because of a blood clot on the brain; the hallucinations, of course, are really angelic visits from Conductor 71.

In an interesting twist, the scenes that take place on Earth are photographed in sumptuous three-strip Technicolor (on one of his visits to Earth to convince Peter to return with him to Heaven, Conductor 71 sighs, "Ah, Technicolor! We're so starved for it up there!") while the scenes in Heaven are shot in black and white. This makes for a curious juxtaposition of earthly and paradisiacal imagery; while Heaven is seen as a largely bureaucratic and impersonal place, with an enormous filing system tracking every person on Earth, the real world is bursting with color, vibrancy, and life—a place that no one would want to leave.

20. Kim Hunter, center in rear, and David Niven, in flying suit, are judged by the court of Heaven in Michael Powell and Emeric Pressburger's *A Matter of Life and Death* (a k a *Stairway to Heaven*, 1946). Photograph courtesy of The Jerry Ohlinger Archives.

Matters are further complicated when Dr. Reeves is killed in a motorcycle accident on his way to surgery to remove the clot from Peter's brain; now in Heaven, Reeves looks on as Peter's surgery proceeds without the doctor's assistance, and Peter's life hangs in the balance (hence the original British title). The film takes a curious turn in its final sequence, a battle-of-the-cultures between Britain and America, touching on the abolishment of the class system in America and the fact that the British citizen lives in a constitutional monarchy while the U.S. is a democracy. In sum, the film demonstrates the feeling of many British citizens during the Second World War that American culture was vulgar, unrefined, and overemotional. The prosecution derides contemporary American culture (a radio spouting jumping jive music magically appears as evidence for the prosecution, as proof of American artistic depravity), while Dr. Reeves, for the defense, argues that the cultural differences between the U.K. and the U.S. have been exaggerated and should be put to rest. He offers one of June's tears (as she prays for Peter's recovery) as proof of the couple's love.

In the film's climax, Peter is granted a generous reprieve and is allowed to live out his life with June in an earthly paradise. *Stairway to Heaven* is a typically lavish film from Powell and Pressburger (known professionally as the Archers) that deals in metaphoric fashion with the exigencies of wartime and makes a plea for American and British postwar cooperation, although the film was begun when the war still raged in Europe. Peculiarly idiosyncratic and very much an auteurist work, *Stairway to Heaven* nevertheless presents a typically efficient picture of wartime Heaven: orderly, neat, free of strife, existing in a world beyond human comprehension and care.

Spencer Williams's *The Blood of Jesus* (1941) is an altogether different affair. *Stairway to Heaven* was designed for white audiences, and presented a decidedly segregated vision of the world beyond. One of the uses of

Heaven that the cinema should be projecting is as a realm of life after death that admits everyone, regardless of race. The lily-white world of *Stairway to Heaven* will not admit to any other ethnicity than that of Anglo-Saxon; indeed, the film's chief conflict derives from the cultural differences between the U.S. and the U.K. in wartime, rather than any suggestion that racial tensions within the armed forces during the period were reshaping the way that American blacks viewed themselves. In Britain, black GIs found a much warmer welcome than they enjoyed in their own hometowns in the Southern United States; indeed, the experience exposed them for the first time to the possibilities of true racial equality. But none of this is examined in *Stairway to Heaven*; it was left to Spencer Williams in *The Blood of Jesus* to actualize paradise for African Americans, and to do so under the most draconian circumstances. Where *Stairway to Heaven* had nearly unlimited resources at its disposal, *The Blood of Jesus* was produced for the astoundingly low sum of $5,000 as an all-African American cast "race movie," in an era in which blacks were denied any effective agency in the Hollywood cinema. Transgressive reinscription is still necessary when one goes to the cinema, as the dominant cinema remains predominantly white and even contemporary audiences of color are inevitably forced to project themselves onto the white performers they see on the screen, out of social and cultural necessity. Contemporary African American stars such as Halle Berry, Denzel Washington, Morgan Freeman, Eddie Murphy, Wesley Snipes, Angela Bassett, and others remind us that an alternative vision is available, if we would only seek it out. In 1941 such a notion was unthinkable in the mainstream cinema. Williams, an actor, writer, and director, ironically was most famous for his work in the brutally racist television series *Amos 'n' Andy* as Andrew Hogg Brown (Andy), which ran on CBS for seventy-eight episodes from June 28, 1951, to June 11, 1953, and then in syndication for many years after, until thankfully protests by the NAACP and other groups forced it off the air.

In the 1940s Williams directed a series of "race" films, designed for African American audiences, which played in cities throughout the

United States in separate theaters that were designated as being for "colored" patrons only, such as *Marching On!* (1943), a paean to the war effort; *Of One Blood* (1944); *Go Down Death* (1946); and *Dirty Gertie from Harlem U.S.A.* (1946), an uncredited version of W. Somerset Maugham's famous short story "Rain." As an actor Williams appeared in numerous short films, stretching back to the early sound films *Music Hath Harms* (Walter Graham, 1929) and *Melancholy Dame* (Arvid E. Gillstrom, 1928), which were designed primarily for white audiences as "novelty" items. With his first directorial work, *The Blood of Jesus* in 1941, Williams was determined to make feature films for *his* audiences on issues that they cared about and could identify with. African American religious filmmaking had a long history going back to the films of Eloise and James Gist, who used their film *Hellbound Train* (1930) as part of her revivalist tent show. Gist was, as Thomas Cripps notes, a

> traveling black preacher. She ranged over the South during the Great Depression, spreading her revivalist faith through motion pictures shot only for the specific narrow purpose defined by her own faith and spirit. Nowhere from script to screen did any white hand intrude, or any white eye observe. Neither white financing in the beginning nor white appreciation at the end affected her pristine black fundamentalism. Her films were naïve, technically primitive, literal depictions of black Southern religious folklore that brought faith to life, much as an illuminated manuscript gave visual life to Christian lore in the Middle Ages. (1979, 4)

Continuing on in this tradition in *The Blood of Jesus,* Williams cast himself as the atheist ne'er-do-well Ras Jackson, an errant husband more interested in drinking and gambling than domesticity until one day he accidentally shoots his devoutly Baptist wife, Martha (Cathryn Caviness), with his hunting rifle while cleaning it in his typically clumsy manner. As historian Mark Deming relates, after the near fatal shooting, Martha's "spirit leaves her body, transported to the Crossroads between Heaven and Hell. There, Martha is tempted from the path of righteousness by Judas Green (Frank H. McClennan), a smooth-talking demon sent by Satan (James B. Jones) who introduces her to the pleasures of liquor and dancing and tries to talk her into a new career as a nightclub hostess, before she realizes that she has begun to travel the path of sin and degradation."

Economies abound in the production, as one might expect for a film made for such a small sum. The cast, for the most part, are nonprofessionals. The film was shot on "short ends" of recanned film stock bought on the "gray market" to save money, with some of the sections of film running less than fifty feet, or roughly thirty seconds of screen time, in 35mm format at the standard sound speed of twenty-four frames per second. The sound recording is poor, and to suggest Heaven, Williams was forced to use stock footage from an early silent film by Georges Méliès (Jones 50) to depict Martha's vision of paradise. In one scene, after Ras enters a room, leaving the door ajar, an anonymous hand emerges from off-screen left and pulls the door shut without any explanation—a no-cost way to preserve continuity. The devil in the film drives a rundown flatbed truck, urging stray souls to "hop inside" for a ride to Hell, an interesting and thrifty approach to depicting Satan's search for new conquests. Much of the film was shot silent, with music and effects added later, and synchronization is often uncertain. The photography is muddy and undistinguished, and scenes in the nightclub and, especially, the house of Ras and Martha, use only the merest suggestions of sets.

Given the film's budget of $5,000, it would be ridiculous to criticize such production shortcomings; it is simply a miracle in its own right that the film was completed. The look of the finished film is thus very rough, but *The Blood of Jesus* resonated with its audiences to an unprecedented degree. An enormous success when released, the film went on to make a fortune for its white producer, Alfred Sack, who promptly signed up Williams to create eight more films for his production company, Sack Amusement Enterprises. As G. William Jones notes, "Williams was able to find in Sack a hands-off backer who enabled him to do what few . . . black artists other than [filmmaker] Oscar Micheaux had been able to do—to direct his screenplays as he saw fit" (34), all of them financial successes at the box office. But *The Blood of Jesus* stood out from the rest of Williams's films for its direct depiction of faith and the sincerity with which it was produced. As Alfred Sack noted years after the film's initial release, *The Blood of Jesus* "was possibly the most successful of all the Negro films and lived the longest . . . and possessed that certain chemistry required by the Negro box office" (qtd. in Cripps 1979, 99). In 1991, fifty years after it was produced, Spencer Williams's "Mighty Epic of Modern Morals!" (the film's tagline) was added to the National Film Registry of the Library of Congress as one of the essential films of twentieth-century cinema.

Marc Connelly and William Keighley's biblically themed film *The Green Pastures* (1936) is a much more traditional and paternalistically racist approach to the subject of religion in the African American community. Based on Connelly's hit Broadway musical, *The Green Pastures* (which won the Pulitzer Prize as a play in 1930), the film is essentially an all-black-cast version written from the viewpoint of a condescending albeit well-meaning white playwright, content to traffic in the most blatant racial stereotypes. Connelly's vision of the American black community was thus precisely the sort of "bland, happy vehicle" that Hollywood was searching for in their treatment of African Americans on the screen. Shooting on studio sets on a relatively lavish budget, Connelly, a neophyte as a film director, received assistance from longtime Warner Bros. contract director William Keighley, whose other credits for the studio included *The Man Who Came to Dinner* (1942), another stage adaptation; together, Keighley and Connelly crafted a safe, racist, predictable vision of African American religious practice in which the Bible is introduced as a series of parables in a Sunday school setting.

Nevertheless, *The Green Pastures* still managed to offend a number of white Southern viewers, simply by the fact that it depicted God ("De Lawd," played by Rex Ingram) as an African American. Indeed,

21. Rex Ingram, as De Lawd, issues instructions to his angels in Marc Connelly and William Keighley's *The Green Pastures* (1936). Photograph courtesy of The Jerry Ohlinger Archives.

as with all "race" films, *The Green Pastures* exists in an entirely segregated universe in which no whites are present, and all the biblical characters, including Noah (Jack Benny's sidekick, Eddie "Rochester" Anderson), Gabriel (Oscar Polk), Eve (Myrtle Anderson), and Adam (Rex Ingram again; he also played the fiery Hezdrel in the film, thus tackling three roles within the project) are African American, which gave the film the air of a "novelty," acceptable in most quarters simply because of the utter absence of any racial diversity.

Connelly's play, based on Roark Bradford's equally patronizing novel *Ol' Man Adam and His Chillun'*, depicts a safely distanced alternative universe in which racial integration is an impossibility, and the actions of the film's protagonists (with the exception of Rex Ingram's "De Lawd") are seen as naïve and infantile. In the world of *The Green Pastures*, the Old Testament becomes a book of children's stories, illustrated in the most simplistic manner. Yet this artificial "innocence" won the film plaudits in many quarters (*Film Daily* voted it one of the top ten films of 1936) even as it was banned in the American South, England, and a number of other foreign countries for being both sacrilegious and offensive to public sensibilities. In the United States more perceptive African American critics also critiqued the film; Roi Ottley, writing in the *Amsterdam News*, denounced the film for its "false sense of values" (Cripps 1977, 260–261), while critic Ralph Matthews, writing in the *African-American* at the time of the film's release, described the film as "a disgrace to the movie industry and a reflection of the colored race" (Cripps 1977, 260).

The Green Pastures was not a success at the box office, due in no small part to the various boycotts against it. Since Warner Bros. had paid $100,000 to acquire the rights to Connolly's play alone (Cripps 1977, 261), to say nothing of the film's production costs, and despite a vigorous studio publicity campaign in the Northern states, the film failed to do significant business. In the wake of the film's failure, it was not until 1943 that MGM made one more attempt at a Hollywood vision of the African American religious experience with Vincente Minnelli's *Cabin in the Sky*, a lavish religious musical with Ethel Waters, Eddie "Rochester" Anderson, Lena Horne, Louis Armstrong, Rex Ingram, Mantan Moreland, and many of the cast members of *The Green Pastures*. Aware of the black community's dissatisfaction with the earlier film, however, MGM producer Arthur Freed promised that "more than ever before we are aware of the Negro problem and are daily moving toward a better understanding. One that in the end will result in a dignified presentation of a peace-loving and loyal people. . . . I will spare nothing and will put everything behind it. It will be a picture on a par with any major film under the M-G-M banner" (qtd. in Parish 42). But despite Freed's apparent good intentions and the genuine sensitivity of Minnelli's direction, *Cabin in the Sky* was yet another hermetically sealed white paean to separatism, racism, and segregation, reflecting the social inequities of the era (or "the Negro problem," as Freed put it) more than anything else, in its tale of shiftless Little Joe (Anderson), his faithful wife Petunia (Waters), and the heavenly battle for Joe's soul as a result of his addiction to gambling. Though presented as a metaphoric battle between the powers of Heaven and Hell for Little Joe's soul, the conclusion of *Cabin in the Sky* shows the audience that the entire affair has been one of Joe's dreams, or more properly nightmares, which drives him to renounce his sinful ways (Parish 43).

Taking place in another, if equally racially segregated, sector of the heavenly domain, Ernst Lubitsch's *Heaven Can Wait* (1943), one of the director's last films, tells the story of Henry Van Cleve (Don Ameche), an amiable philanderer on Earth, who is summoned to a final reckoning with Satan (the corpulent 1940s villain Laird Cregar, known as "His Excellency" in the film), who will decide whether Van Cleve will spend eternity in Heaven or Hell. An inveterate womanizer, Henry is certain that his damnation is assured, but as he recounts the story of his life to Satan it emerges that (at least in Lubitsch's view) Henry Van Cleve is simply "human, all too human" and not guilty of any serious breach of conduct that would permanently consign him to the flames of Hell. During the course of Henry's recitation, various other supplicants appear before His Excellency, all assuring him blithely that they have been "sent to the wrong place through a frightful misunderstanding," but His Excellency will tolerate none of their excuses and with the push of a button exiles them all to perdition. But Van Cleve's frank admission of his "sins" intrigues Satan; Henry assures him that unlike with the others there has been "no mistake" and that he is perfectly prepared to accept his punishment. Indeed, Henry Van Cleve is a fitting candidate for damnation by the standards of Western Christian theology; he is, as critic Richard Scheib points out, "a rampant womanizer, a liar, a cheat, [and] an adulterer . . . beginning with his French tutor at the age of fifteen, then stealing and marrying [his] cousin's fiancée on the eve of their wedding, [and continuing on to] the flings he still carried on with beautiful women throughout his marriage and into his old age."

It is not too much to say that in *Heaven Can Wait,* Lubitsch is reviewing his own life as a sexual adventurer, and that perhaps he identified to some degree with Henry Van Cleve's self-doubts and was wrestling with his own mortality (Lubitsch would die of a heart attack on November 30, 1947). As a Continental sophisticate, although he closely tailored his work for the American public, Lubitsch was much more in sympathy with the European attitude toward human sexuality and social conventions. Thus, the final moment of *Heaven Can Wait,* in which His Excellency puts Van Cleve on an elevator and instructs the operator to send him "up" to Heaven, might well be read as Lubitsch's own wish to be forgiven for whatever fleshly transgressions he had committed in his life. There is very little of Heaven or Hell in *Heaven Can Wait;* most of the action is confined to His Excellency's antechamber, where Henry relates his life story in a series of flashbacks. Nevertheless, the dichotomy of Heaven or Hell dominates the film's mise-en-scène as the consequence of a series of conscious decisions that one makes in one's life. Lubitsch's vision is one of tolerance and forgiveness, and a trifle self-centered in the final analysis. Henry Van Cleve's transgressions are clearly seen by the film as forgivable human foibles, in contrast to the more serious sins of greed, vanity, and violence, which are dealt with by His Excellency without a moment's hesitation.

Oddly enough, Alexander Hall's celestial fantasy *Here Comes Mr. Jordan* (1941) was based on a play entitled *Heaven Can Wait* by Harry Segall, but had nothing to do with Lubitsch's film; to further complicate matters, *Here Comes Mr. Jordan* was remade in 1978 by Warren Beatty and Buck Henry as *Heaven Can Wait.* Yet the tale of reincarnation and angelic intercession told in both *Here Comes Mr. Jordan* and the 1978 *Heaven Can Wait* bears no resemblance to the narrative of Lubitsch's 1943 film. Indeed, *Here Comes Mr. Jordan* proceeds from an entirely different set of assumptions. Boxer Joe Pendleton (Robert Montgomery) is killed in a plane crash, but his death, as was Peter Carter's in *Stairway to Heaven*, is the result of a celestial oversight by novice angel Messenger 7013 (Edward Everett Horton). Before Pendleton can be restored to his body it is cremated, forcing the angelic Mr. Jordan (Claude Rains) to offer Joe a new body, that of recently deceased millionaire Bruce Farnsworth, who has conveniently just been drowned by his grasping wife, Julia (Rita Johnson), and her devious private secretary, Tony Abbott (John Emery). As Farnsworth, Joe is able to use his position to right several wrongs that Farnsworth has committed during his business career, most notably against the father of Bette Logan (Evelyn Keyes), whom Farnsworth had framed in a securities swindle.

Predictably, Joe/Bruce falls in love with Bette and uses Farnsworth's millions to save her father from disgrace. This, however, is too much for Julia and Tony, who once again murder Farnsworth, leaving Joe to search for a new body. Reincarnated for a final time as Ralph "KO" Murdoch, a boxer who has been shot for refusing to throw a fight, Joe wins a championship fight, loses his memory of his life as Joe, and "becomes" Murdoch, who, in the final moments of the film, meets and falls in love with Bette without remembering their earlier romance.

The theme of angelic intervention in human affairs remains astonishingly popular, as evidenced by the success of such recent television series as *Touched by an Angel*. The wide-ranging series of films in which angels figure as agents of social change include Ben Hecht and Charles MacArthur's *The Scoundrel* (1935), where the ghost of ruthless publisher Anthony Mallare (Noël Coward) returns to Earth to atone for his vicious disregard of others during his professional career; when at last his task is accomplished, Mallare is allowed to enter into Heaven. In Frank Capra's *It's a Wonderful Life* (1946), the bumbling angel Clarence Oddbody (Henry Travers) is sent to Earth to help George Bailey (James Stewart) as he struggles to find his place in small-town American society, complete with a reassuring ending that emphasizes community values versus the greed of rampant capitalism as presented in the person of Mr. Potter (Lionel Barrymore), the miserly proprietor of the local bank; Clarence the angel, meanwhile, is rewarded for his efforts on Earth by winning his wings in Heaven. Playing another, more dapper angel is Cary Grant as Dudley, who comforts the loveless Julia Brougham (Loretta Young) in Henry Koster's *The Bishop's Wife* (1947); Clifton Webb and Edmund Gwenn appear as angels in George Seaton's *For Heaven's Sake* (1950), once again dispatched to solve the problems of mere mortals; Clarence Brown's *Angels in the Outfield* (1951) deploys angels to help the Pittsburgh Pirates win the National League Pennant; angel Billy Bigelow (Gordon MacRae) returns to Earth to assist his family in Henry King's version of the Broadway musical *Carousel* (1956); and Harry Belafonte appears as Alexander, *The Angel Levine*, in Ján Kadár's eponymous film of 1970, to assist poor, elderly tailor Morris Mishkin (Zero Mostel), who can no longer care for himself, his business, or his seriously ill wife, Fanny (Ida Kaminska), and to restore hope and happiness to the couple, who are naturally surprised by the angel's sudden appearance in the family kitchen.

Jerry Zucker's enormously successful *Ghost* (1990) offers Patrick Swayze as Sam Wheat, a decent man who is murdered by a mugger but remains on Earth to protect his fiancée, Molly Jensen (Demi Moore), from the predatory advances of their supposed friend Carl Bruner (Tony Goldwyn), who had actually ordered Sam's murder. With the aid of medium Oda Mae Brown (Whoopi Goldberg), Sam exposes Carl's treachery and in a climactic fight accidentally kills Carl. Carl's body is promptly dragged off to Hell for his various misdeeds, while Sam, after professing his love for Molly, vanishes into Heaven in a blaze of white light. (See Parish for more examples of this curious "angelic" subgenre.)

In life, we like to think that the guilty will be punished and the virtuous rewarded; this is the essence of all religious mythology. And yet the mechanics of Heaven remain obscure. The conventional Hollywood cinema, with few exceptions, is not involved in an excavation of the genesis or spiritual basis of the concepts of paradise or eternal damnation; the occasional film that does examine these belief systems in detail, such as Pier Paolo Pasolini's *The Gospel According to St. Matthew* (*Il vangelo secondo Matteo*, 1964), operates outside the dominant cinema and is often the work of interested but ultimately uninvolved nonbelievers. Shooting on location in Italy, using nonsynchronous sound (the dialogue was dubbed in later) and employing for the most part a cast of dedicated nonprofessionals, Pasolini created a sensuously black-and-white "newsreel" account of Christ's brief time on Earth, casting the magnetic Enrique Irazoqui, then a young Catalan student of economics, in the leading role to great effect. Pasolini's Christ is not so much a gentle shepherd as a stern prophet, who delivers a series of striking warnings to the populace, is not afraid to take direct action when it is necessary, and radiates a sense of purpose and determination in all his actions.

For the most part, the dominant cinema uses Heaven as a location for atonement, a device to reunite separated lovers, a temporary waystation from which one can depart at will to return to Earth to intervene in human affairs, a bucolic Edenic paradise that, regardless of one's beliefs, offers an eternity of spiritual peace, reunion with loved ones, and freedom from the material strife of corporeal existence.

In Sutton Vane's play *Outward Bound*, first filmed by Robert Milton under its original title in 1930 and then remade as *Between Two Worlds* by Edward A. Blatt in 1944, a group of people find themselves on board a mysterious ocean liner bound for Heaven or Hell. In the 1930 version, the protagonists are Ann (Helen Chandler) and Henry (Douglas Fairbanks, Jr.), two lovers who have attempted suicide by gas rather than renounce their illicit romance, with Dudley Digges as Thompson, the "Examiner" who will determine their fates. In the 1944 version, John Garfield and Eleanor Parker play the doomed couple, Tom and Ann, but the action has been updated to wartime London. In both *Between Two Worlds* and *Outward Bound*, the lovers are joined by a cross

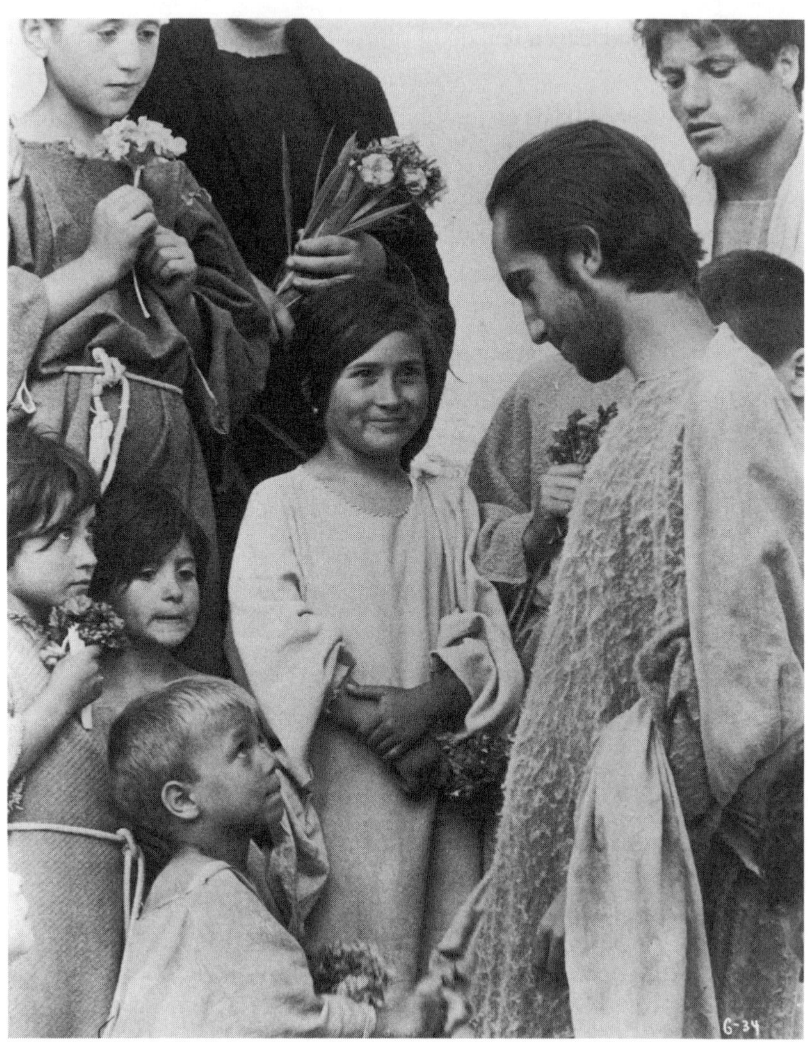

22. Enrique Irazoqui as Christ speaks to the children of his followers in Pier Paolo Pasolini's *The Gospel According to St. Matthew* (1964). Photograph courtesy of The Jerry Ohlinger Archives.

section of humanity, as in Alfred Hitchcock's famous wartime parable *Lifeboat* (1944). *Between Two Worlds* offers Sydney Greenstreet as the Reverend Tim Thompson, the mysterious Examiner, and Edmund Gwenn as Scrubby, the ship's steward, who tries to keep the passengers ignorant of the true purpose of their journey.

None of the passengers on the fog-bound ship can remember how they got there; they only know that they are drifting toward some unknown destination. One by one, the truth sinks in; this is really a voyage across the river Styx, and Stubby is Charon, the boatman who will guide them to the afterlife. When the true nature of their journey becomes apparent, some of the passengers panic and try to bargain their way out, most notably the millionaire industrialist Lingley (George Coulouris). The Examiner, however, is unmoved by his threats, bribes, and blandishments. For the lovers, Tom and Ann, however, there is a happier fate. Convinced of the stupidity of their attempted suicide, they are returned to their gas-filled London flat as a conveniently timed shell fragment explodes through a window, allowing the gas to escape. The lovers have received a second chance; the film implies that we are each responsible for our own destiny and must soldier on in the face of adversity, as the responsibility of the living.

Reginald LeBorg's *The Flight That Disappeared* (1961) offers a similar moral fable for the Cold War era. On a transcontinental flight from Los Angeles to Washington, D.C., a nuclear scientist, an expert on rocketry, and a mathematical genius are suddenly transported from their normal flight path into a stratospheric climb ten miles above the earth. When the plane finally comes to rest in a nest of clouds, the three scientists leave the plane and its other passengers (who have seemingly lapsed into a coma), to be judged by an otherworldly tribunal for their involvement in creating a new and terrible atomic weapon, the Beta Bomb. The two chief designers of the device, Dr. Carl Morris (Dayton Lummis) and Tom Endicott (Craig Hill), are put on trial in a zone that is "beyond space or time" and shown the potential results of their work, in a world ravaged by famine, destruction, and war.

As the tribunal's chief examiner (Gregory Morton) concludes his indictment, the three men agree that the Beta Bomb potentially promises to destroy mankind. Their ethereal advocate (Addison Richards), speaking for all the "future beings of the world," argues that the scientists should be released on condition that the results of the work never reach fruition. Returning to the plane, the men are transported back to Earth as the other passengers regain consciousness. Saying nothing to the others of their experience with the tribunal, the scientists destroy the plans for the Beta Bomb after landing in Washington and agree to lie to the president and his advisors about the outcome of their research. As far as the world will ever know, the project has ended in failure, which paradoxically is a victory for the future of civilization. A deeply personal work by LeBorg, who had earlier made the proto-feminist *Destiny* (1944) from footage excised from co-

23. Nuclear scientists face a heavenly tribunal in Reginald LeBorg's *The Flight That Disappeared* (1961). Photograph courtesy of The Jerry Ohlinger Archives.

director Julien Duvivier's *Flesh and Fantasy* (1943), it was enhanced with new material shot in a matter of days to complete the project, such that *The Flight That Disappeared* is perhaps the least expensive film discussed in this chapter (with the exception of *The Blood of Jesus*), with a shooting schedule of less than a week and a budget of less than $100,000.

The visions of paradise offered in the films discussed here all share one common trait: they argue for the existence of Heaven, or paradise, as a real and tangible domain, not something to be taken on faith. It is comforting to believe that paradise does exist, if only because it makes our quotidian existence on Earth all the more acceptable; a better world lies ahead. The visions of paradise offered in Alice Guy's *The Life of Christ*, Cecil B. DeMille's silent version of *The King of Kings* (1927), Mervyn LeRoy's *Quo Vadis?* (1951), Henry Koster's *The Robe* (1953), William Wyler's *Ben-Hur* (1959), Nicholas Ray's *King of Kings* (1961), Norman Jewison's *Jesus Christ, Superstar* (1973), Jean-Luc Godard's modern retelling *Hail Mary* (*Je vous salue, Marie*, 1985), Martin Scorsese's *The Last Temptation of Christ* (1988), and Mel Gibson's *The Passion of the Christ* (2004) all share one factor in common: they depict a world beyond our own, in which all debts have been settled, all transactions completed, all wrongs brought to final account (see Kinnard and Davis). Heaven, or paradise, is the ultimate zone of escape from the ephemeral reality of corporeal existence, a place that allows us freedom without limits. In the final chapter of this volume, I will turn to space as "the final frontier" of human experience, offering a paradise of its own, a place to begin again, a world without end.

CHAPTER FIVE

The Promise of the Future

All science fiction, by definition, takes place in the future. If the technology is not available now, then it has to be invented; this is something that will happen in another time, another era, but not now. The promise of the future is that new technologies will continue to be developed as the old ones fall away; fossil fuel technology will give way to a world powered by solar cells, clean nuclear energy, cold fusion, and the like. When one looks back on the 1950s "populuxe" films of what the future would hold for the average family, one sees flying saucers routinely used for commuting to work, monorails and flying platforms for mass transit, and prefab houses that assemble themselves in a matter of seconds. But the most pervasive image in this fiberglass world is not an image at all, but rather the absence of want, poverty, starvation, war, and human misery. Our bodies will be endlessly renewable, there will be more than enough food for the entire world to eat, and war will have been abolished. Such dystopian fantasies as Elio Petri's *The 10th Victim* (*La decima vittima*, 1965) propose that war will have been outlawed in favor of "The Hunt," in which those who persist in violent activities are paired off into "hunters" and "victims" in a series of ritual stalkings for cash prizes, while the rest of the populace relaxes, secure in the knowledge that global conflict is a thing of the past. Yet the world of *The 10th Victim* is not without its drawbacks; as in Michael Anderson's *Logan's Run* (1976), the elderly are dispatched forthwith as having outlived their usefulness, and books have been replaced by comic-book versions of the original—who has time to read? But the promise of the future ultimately is that of infinite change, in which one technology is replaced by another in a relentless parade of invention and improvement, a future that we can see rapidly evolving in front of our eyes today as VHS tapes are replaced by DVDs and then memory chips and Tivo, as our dreams of the future are stored in hard-drive memories to be replayed, freeze-framed, and ultimately erased to make way for the new dream of the future. The future is a zone for perpetual re-creation; the promise of the future is that it will someday become the present.

When Worlds Collide (Rudolph Maté, 1951) begins with a startling premise. A rogue star has been discovered hurtling toward Earth, and in a matter of months, it will annihilate humankind's domain. Its sister planet, Zyra, will pass Earth at close range but will effect no real destruction. As is usually the case with such doomsday scenarios, the scientists who recognize the danger are ridiculed by the public at large. Despite the public's lack of faith in their pronouncements, Dr. Cole Hendron (Larry Keating) and his associates convince avaricious multimillionaire Sydney Stanton (John Hoyt at his most unpleasant) to back their project: the creation of a rocket ship to carry a small group of survivors to where the atmosphere seems much like that of our home planet. Stanton's motives for financing the project are simple: he wants to be one of the forty-four people to journey to the new world of Zyra, along with a veritable Noah's Ark of flora and fauna. Confined to a wheelchair, Stanton rails against Dr. Hendron and his colleagues, accusing them of being "crackpots" even as he urges them to proceed at top speed in the construction of the experimental rocket. Hendron assembles a huge construction crew, and in less than eight months, the ship is ready for its one and only flight. However, not everyone can fit on the rocket ship; the passengers are chosen by a lottery and by their physical and mental capabilities. At the last possible moment, it is discovered that the fuel calculations are slightly off and more passengers will have to be jettisoned. Those not chosen for the journey start a riot, as Stanton had predicted from the outset, demanding to be taken to the new world. Sacrificing both himself and the furious Stanton, Dr. Hendron refuses to board the spaceship, thus assuring it of sufficient fuel to reach the new Eden. As the ship glides into outer space on a gigantic ramp, we witness the destruction of Earth in a series of cataclysmic tidal waves, exploding volcanoes, and raging fires.

But as viewers, we see the destruction of a curiously depeopled space, in which buildings, glaciers, mountains, and cities are reduced to rubble without any human referent. When Manhattan is buried beneath a tidal wave, there are no screams, no people desperate to escape. The earth dies silently, even as Dr. Hendron's rocket ship streaks on through space. It is as if the world had never really existed at all and is disposed of without a backward glance. When the spaceship glides to a stop on Zyra, the all-white passengers and crew file out into a new world where they can begin life again.

The novel *When Worlds Collide* by Philip Wylie and Edwin Balmer on which the film was based had once been considered by the spectacle-obsessed Cecil B. DeMille as a possible film project, and the overtly religious tone of the narrative reflects the hyper-Christianity of the 1950s, a mood that is reflected in today's social discourse. Indeed, it is strongly implied at the film's opening that the world is simply too sinful to exist. A biblical quotation effectively frames the film's narrative: "And God looked down upon the Earth and beheld it was corrupt, for all flesh has corrupted His way upon the Earth." Thus the earth's destruction is viewed by the film as more than justified; it's time to start with a clean slate and a sweeping exclusion of all cultures other than white Anglo-Saxon Protestants.

Perhaps the most shocking aspect of the film is the manner in which it erases racial and social difference by refusing to even acknowledge its existence. The forty survivors who land on Zyra momentarily speculate on whether or not they should don oxygen masks as they venture out onto the verdant pastures of their new home, but decide against it. After all, as one of the passengers asks, where else are they to go? But Zyra does not disappoint; a sun-drenched meadow, spotted with exotic flowers and vegetation, awaits our intrepid band of travelers and their passable managers. Zyra will be their new home, where they will reproduce and flourish, a location devoid of sin, or human history, or racial, national, and international boundaries and their concomitant conflicts.

Showing Zyra's new residents as all identical as they descend the ship's gangplank in heterotopic pairs, *When Worlds Collide* posits the creation of a new theocratic state open only to those who inherit through divine providence—much like the concept of "the Rapture" embraced by evangelical Christians, whose cars bear bumper stickers emblazoned with the slogan "Warning! Occupants of this vehicle may vanish at any moment!" thus identifying themselves as expecting to be among the saved who will be assimilated into the heavens, when the time comes, by a very angry and deeply judgmental deity. In *When Worlds Collide*, it is not the people but Earth itself that vanishes, leaving only a chosen few to repopulate a new, ethnically cleansed world. Today these elisions seem obvious, or at least they should. In the 1950s, with the risk of nuclear war hanging over the world, the public seemed eager for an end to the seemingly ceaseless conflict, and *When Worlds Collide* offered just such a spectacle. Unlike the similarly themed *War of the Worlds* (1953), in which Earth is saved at the last moment by God's intervention in the form of viruses that humans have become resistant to, but which are fatal to the poorly immunized Martian invaders, in *When Worlds Collide*, Earth is "saved" through destruction. What will transpire on Zyra as the new age dawns? The film ends on a note of boundless optimism, and yet Eden may still prove to be treacherous; who knows what conflicts among the survivors might yet arise?

The Edenic search in *When Worlds Collide* is not only a matter of seeking a potential Utopia, but also a search for simple survival. The earth, our home, has ceased to exist, and on board the rocket ship to Zyra there is no going back; our point of origin has been erased. Thus only the goal suffices; any effort that does not culminate in success is a gesture toward complete oblivion—the earth and all its inhabitants gone. *When Worlds Collide*, taken in a more abstract sense, also suggests the conflict between the artificial structures of civilization and the impulse to return to a more natural way of living, in closer harmony with the earth's life force.

Alternatively, paradise can rise out of the ashes of a dead civilization, out of the ruins of a planet devastated by nuclear war. Edward Bernds's *World Without End* (1956) is both a cautionary tale and an Edenic saga. When the crew of a rocket ship accidentally break through the time barrier on the way to the first manned landing on Mars, they find themselves back at their point of origin, on Earth, but in the year 2508. Centuries of war have left the earth decimated and largely uninhabitable; the astronauts realize that their ship has been damaged beyond repair and there is no hope of returning to the past. There is only one thing to do: as in *When Worlds Collide*, the astronauts resolve to begin life anew, and gathering together the few remaining members of the population unaffected by radiation sickness, they set about the task of schooling a new generation in the arts, sciences, and literature, rebuilding society from the ground up. There are other survivors of the final meteor war, as well: mutants who live like animals and prey upon the healthy survivors. The crew helps the unaffected members of society to defeat their Paleolithic counterparts and begin a school, find fresh water, and institute rudimentary forms of democratic social government. The film ends with these final hopeful images as the new society takes hold, still too primitive to begin again the process of destroying itself, offering a new and verdant world for all its citizens.

An even more unusual vision of an Edenic future society is offered in Harry Horner's *Red Planet Mars* (1952), which is usually cited as one of the classic Red Scare films of the McCarthy era. Scientist Chris Cronyn (Peter Graves) is obsessed with contacting the planet Mars from his idyllic mountain laboratory; much to his surprise, one evening the planet responds to Cronyn's broadcasts with a passage from the Bible. The broadcast, however, does not actually originate on Mars; instead, it emanates from the mountaintop outpost of ex-Nazi scientist Franz Calder (Herbert Berghof), now employed by the Stalinist regime as an agent of Soviet domination. Calder, furious over the appropriation of his numerous inventions by the West in the wake of the Allied victory in World War II, is aiding the Soviets because it suits his personal desire for revenge and because, as an atheist, he feels that any form of religious worship is a contemptible symptom of American weakness.

The film's most bizarre twist comes when God actually begins broadcasting holy admonitions from Mars, bringing about a religious revolution in Russia that overthrows the Communist regime. Fleeing the collapsing Soviet Union, Berghof travels to Cronyn's observatory and tells Cronyn and his wife, Linda (Andrea King), that he will inform the world that the majority of the "religious messages" have been fakes, perpetuated by the disgruntled scientist as an act of malicious interference. Berghof is understandably astonished when God steps in with genuine broadcasts, but still plans to go public with the details of his fraudulent scheme. The Cronyns prevent this, however, by intentionally blowing up their laboratory, killing themselves and Berghof, thus assuring that his deception will never be discovered. For all the world knows, *all* the evangelical admonitions are genuine, and the United States and Russia enter the mid-1950s as partners in theist world peace.

Taken as a serious social statement when first released, today *Red Planet Mars* is both a cinematic and social curiosity. The film ends with an image of the Cronyns' children, now safely in the White House with the president (Willis Bouchey), gazing out the windows of the Oval Office into the sunbeam-streaked dawn of a new era as one of the chief executive's aides (an uncredited Walter Sande) intones in solemn awe, "You're his children," conflating Cronyn's work with God's last-minute intervention to save the planet from Berghof's untimely revelations. While most of the Cold War artifacts of this period have been suppressed because of changing social attitudes, *Red Planet Mars* remains a popular title, often revived as one of the more bizarre exemplars of a nation in social and spiritual crisis.

The same sense of Cold War hysteria also pervades William Wellman's equally bizarre *The Next Voice You Hear . . .* (1950), in which God's voice is heard on the radio for six consecutive nights, essentially delivering a celestial "pep talk" to a world weary of war and human suffering. As might be expected, though the phenomenon is worldwide, the film centers its action around the impact of God's speeches in America as they directly affect the lives of "Joe Smith, American" (James Whitmore), his wife, Mary (Nancy Davis, later married to Ronald Reagan), and their clean-cut youngster, Johnny (Gary Gray). Joe Smith is an average working stiff, and his life is boring and difficult; he clashes continually with his tyrannical boss, Mr. Brannan (Art Smith) and feels put upon and exploited by those above him socially and financially. God's messages change all that, as He urges His constituents to "take it easy" and learn to get along with one another. Young Johnny vanishes from time to time and his father doesn't know where he is, but it develops that Johnny is *friends* with Mr. Brannan and has been hanging around Brannan's house because unlike with his father, Johnny can really talk with Brannan about things that matter in life. Indeed, Brannan will tell Joe that "Johnny is my friend," and this odd relationship brings about a rapprochement between Joe and Brannan.

Director William Wellman, known as "Wild Bill" in the film capital because of his blunt manner and his habit of carrying a gun around to threaten actors if they misbehaved or slacked off during a production (Wellman's most famous films are *The Public Enemy* [1931], *Wild Boys of the Road* [1933], and *The Light That Failed* [1939]), was an odd choice to direct this film, which was shot on a short schedule and modest budget by producer Dore Schary as a personal project for MGM. Throughout the film we are never allowed to hear God's voice—the narrative always manages to shift to another location before we can actually hear the deity speak—but we are treated to watercooler discussions of His texts the following day as the citizens of the world wonder whether God's intervention in the affairs of mankind heralds the coming of the apocalypse or the dawn of a new era. As the film

24. James Whitmore, as "Joe Smith, American," hears the voice of God on the radio in William Wellman's *The Next Voice You Hear* (1950). Photograph courtesy of The Jerry Ohlinger Archives.

ends, and God's message of "love and brotherhood" takes hold on the world, *The Next Voice You Hear* ... presents the viewer with a world in which labor and capital have been reconciled (much like Fritz Lang's *Metropolis* [1927]), family bonds restored, and countries united in a common search for world peace; in short, paradise on Earth restored.

In this the film bears a curious resemblance to Diane Keaton's much later directorial debut, *Heaven* (1987), in which a group of Keaton's friends and associates ruminate on the nature of Heaven—what it will be like, whether or not it exists, how one can enter Heaven—intercut with clips of the Hollywood "Heavens" described in the last chapter, everything from *Metropolis* to Raoul Walsh's bizarre comedy *The Horn Blows at Midnight* (1945), in which Jack Benny, as a trumpeter in a big band on a radio show, falls asleep during the program and dreams that he is the angel Athanael, sent from Heaven to blow the trumpet blast that will signal the end of the world. In *Heaven*, Keaton's interview subjects are essentially describing a paradise on Earth, which is what *The Next Voice You Hear*... posits as a potential reality—given the aid of divine intervention. Despite its theist trappings, *The Next Voice You Hear*... eventually seems to be more of a science-fiction film than the portent of a religious revival; we never hear God's voice, and thus we have to take the matter on faith. Has God's word really been heard on Earth, or is it a mass hallucination? And why does He need the three radio networks as a means of communication? In the final analysis, *The Next Voice You Hear*... is more an implicit commercial for radio sets in an

25. Jack Benny, center, plays a bumbling angel in Raoul Walsh's *The Horn Blows at Midnight* (1945), with Alexis Smith (as Elizabeth) and Guy Kibbee (as The Chief). Photograph courtesy of The Jerry Ohlinger Archives.

era increasingly dominated by television; perhaps God knows that television will emerge as one of the greatest threats to Hollywood's global hegemony.

In 1939, when affairs in Europe were arguably at their bleakest in the twentieth century, with Hitler on the march in Poland and Czechoslovakia and London bracing for the Blitz, H. G. Wells wrote an essay for a short book entitled *Travels of a Republican Radical in Search of Hot Water.* Never reprinted, the volume contains a key essay for any understanding of Wells as a scenarist and social visionary, "The Honour and Dignity of the Free Mind," which was to have been delivered at the P.E.N. Congress in Stockholm, Sweden, on September 4–7, 1939. The "war crisis," however, forced the cancellation of the congress, so Wells, already in Stockholm, presented the completed essay to "one or two writers who had already gathered there" (Wells 122), hardly the ideal audience for the widest possible dissemination of his work. In the aftermath of the disrupted gathering, Wells coupled his essay with a series of other topical writings and brought it out as a slim paperback volume, offering us the only record of the work that might have been undertaken at the canceled Stockholm conference: the creation of a united defense of artists against the Axis powers. As Wells wrote, with considerable passion,

> Are the creative and intellectual workers, the universities, the teachers, the hunters of knowledge and wisdom to be at the beck and call of obscure government officials obeying the behests and even anticipating the wishes of some gangster adventurer, some financial trickster or some vote-wangling politician; or are they the masters whom it behooves all governments and social organisations to heed and serve? . . . Can there be any doubt among us here of the answer? Is there any question that the imaginative

> and creative brain is the supreme value in human life, and that its freedom and dignity are the primary concern of every civilised man? Is there any question that these belligerent sovereign states which rule us everywhere, their bosses and their officials and their cants, are now an intolerable menace to everything worth while in human life? (132, 150)

These questions had preoccupied Wells for quite some time, certainly since the film adaptation of his prescient novel *The Shape of Things to Come* (shot in 1935, released in 1936), which accurately predicted the outbreak of World War II (although in Wells's vision, the war lasted into the mid-1960s) and ended in a Utopian vision of "the world of the airmen," a global democratic technocracy in which culture, art, and scientific enlightenment were the sole aims of humankind. Stunningly directed by William Cameron Menzies, who three years later would design the entire production of Victor Fleming's *Gone With the Wind* (1939) and in 1953 create the ultimate childhood dystopian nightmare of Cold War alienation, *Invaders from Mars* (1953), *Things to Come* covers nearly a century in human affairs, from 1940 through 2036. John Cabal (Raymond Massey) is a pacifist who opposes war, but as Christmas Eve draws near, in a brutally effective montage juxtaposing traditional holiday merriment with newspaper headlines blaring "WAR IMMINENT!" it is clear that Cabal's hopes for a peaceful world are doomed.

London (named "Everytown" in the film) is bombed into oblivion by unnamed foreign forces, giving rise to a zombie-like plague called "the Wandering Sickness," which robs people of their will and sends them out into the world to murder and pillage. The only cure for the affliction is summary execution, something that the now-ruling "Boss" (Ralph Richardson) is more than willing to mete out to his subjects, even as he presides over the ruin of civilization, without adequate sanitation, food, or medical supplies. The war rages on until 1966, when a certain kind of feudal order uneasily descends upon the earth and its inhabitants. But social government as we know it has collapsed; in

26. The future as utopia in William Cameron Menzies's *Things to Come* (1936). Photograph courtesy of The Jerry Ohlinger Archives.

its place, a group of warring "nation states" fights over the surviving scraps of civilization.

The Boss, indeed, is just another feudal dictator presiding over a corner of the earth, carrying on the centuries-old traditions of conquest, plunder, and dictatorship, despite the feeble efforts of a surviving group of scientists who oppose his reign. All this changes when John Cabal, now much older, arrives with a fleet of massive airplanes as the representative of a new government that is taking over the world. The Boss is soon vanquished by Cabal's superior technology, and "the world of the airmen" takes over, bringing peace and plenty to the citizens of the world. The film then shifts to its final third, in which the "Everytown" in 2036 has been transformed into a paradise of robotic automation, plentiful food and water, enlightened cultural education using television and a forerunner of DVDs as classroom tools, and the hope of sending a man to the moon in the first manned spacecraft.

But with the intellectual freedom offered by the new world, there are those who disagree with the new regime's arms, chief among them the Cassandra-like Theotocopulos (Sir Cedric Hardwicke). Delivering a dramatic warning of doom to the citizens of Everytown via a huge telescreen, Theotocopulos foments a rebellion against the proposed moon flight and leads an assault by a group of malcontents on the landing site, where the rocket is launched moments before Theotocopulos and the members of his mob close in. At the end of the film, Oswald Cabal, John Cabal's great grandson (Raymond Massey in a dual role), heralds the new scientific achievement as the first step in conquering the stars, which he sees as the ultimate destiny of the human race.

While the implied social equality of Wells's vision of the future is highly debatable—the "democracy" of the airmen seems conspicuously sterile, and the vast sets recall the gargantuan buildings of *Metropolis* (1927), which dwarfed their numerous inhabitants—Wells was trying to show that rule by conventional politicians was doomed to failure and suggested that a Utopia created by scientists and artists would have a better chance at realizing human potential. It would be an interesting experiment, if attempted; for the present, the world seems to have learned little from Wells's prophetic vision and seems more divided and war-torn than ever. Indeed, the plethora of otherworldly visitors with benevolent intentions in the history of cinema indicates that we know that, as humans, we are fatally flawed and doomed to repeat the past, ending in our inevitable self-destruction, unless some outside agency (angelic or extraterrestrial) comes to our aid.

Things to Come asks whether or not progress for its own sake is valuable or if it needs to be governed by something other than mere scientific curiosity; that is, by the human conscience. If the march forward into new technological landscapes is inevitable, no matter whether the outcome be salutary or dystopian, *Things to Come* seeks to assure us that we are the masters of our own spiritual, artistic, and technological destinies and that we alone bear the ultimate responsibility for all our actions. While *Things to Come* pays lip service to the concept of a higher power, it ultimately argues that humankind is the highest power, for both good and ill. The question is, what will we do with this freedom, and what kind of world will we create with the aid of technology?

Lothar Mendes's *The Man Who Could Work Miracles* (1936) posits a different question: What would we do if we were able to create, at will, a new civilization; if all our fantasies could become fact merely by wishing them into existence? Based on H. G. Wells's short story, running a mere seven thousand words in its initial incarnation (Wykes 71), *The Man Who Could Work Miracles* tells the story of the very plebeian George McWhirter Fotheringay (Roland Young), who is granted godlike powers by a trio of bored deities (Ivan Brandt, Torin Thatcher, and, in one of his first screen roles, the ineffably bored George Sanders) who argue that men should never be allowed to control their own destinies; they simply don't have the intelligence to manage their own affairs.

In short order, Fotheringay, touched by the hand of the gods, sets out to create a new, Utopian civilization, only to discover that his own vanity and greed have foredoomed the effort. Progressing from a series of insignificant parlor tricks, Fotheringay is soon reordering the entire planet as an absolute monarchy, with himself as the Earth's ruler. Even as the evidence of his miraculous power spreads, Fotheringay is met with a chorus of naysayers, who challenge him to prove his illuminate power once and for all. To do this, Fotheringay orders the earth to stop spinning on its axis, which negates the planet's gravitational pull and nearly brings about the destruction of the Earth. As a last wish, Fotheringay asks that the world be returned to its initial state, before he was given the gift to "work miracles," and that he should return to his life as an average, pub-going British citizen. His wish is granted, and the world is restored. As Alan Wykes observed,

> Wells's great strength as a writer is his ability to interest the reader immediately in what he has to say. His style is straightforward, serviceable, untrimmed with decoration or rhetoric. . . . He was a Common Man himself, he understood poverty, he knew about the dependence of the lower orders on those in the ranks above them; he had views on the emancipation of women at the precise moment when women themselves were probing the same ideas; he made himself a spokesman for the very folk whose interest he was engaging. (16)

The Man Who Could Work Miracles was a resounding success at the box office and touched a chord with the average British citizen with its tale of an everyman given limitless power; a common fantasy to the present day. But in depicting the Utopic world that Fotheringay creates as disintegrating into a feudal dictatorship, Wells was merely repeating one of his favorite arguments: that society must be governed by a political, literary, and scientific elite and not by the artificial dictates of a too-easily-manipulated democracy of average citizens or by a common man raised up by the union of circumstance to the level of dictator.

And yet, at the same time, a number of films from the 1950s seemed to argue that without a guiding, benevolent despot, the world would ultimately fail to reach accord on important social issues and vanish in a cloud of nuclear debris. In these films, aliens arrive on Earth with a warning against self-destruction, but they often have to threaten the world with extinction in order to get sufficient attention.

In Robert Wise's *The Day the Earth Stood Still* (1951), Klaatu (Michael Rennie) comes from outer space to bring a message of peace and harmony to the earth. Posing as a human, "Mr. Carpenter," Klaatu falls in love with Helen Benson (Patricia Neal); when her jealous ex-boyfriend Tom Stevens (Hugh Marlowe) discovers Klaatu's origin, he attempts to turn Klaatu over to the police for investigation and imprisonment. But Klaatu's faithful robot servant Gort (Lock Martin) rescues Klaatu from death when he is shot by the authorities while trying to escape, and he successfully returns to his ship. There, he delivers a warning: Disarm, or perish. As he tells the assembled scientists and government officials, "We shall be waiting for your answer." With this stern admonition Klaatu departs, ending the film on a note of Cold War uncertainty. Will mankind embrace Klaatu's message of nonviolence? Or are we doomed to ceaselessly repeat the past, assuring our inevitable destruction? Klaatu's world of pervasive nonviolence is more perfect than ours can ever be, a world of sanity and reason at odds with the combative, fear-based values of 1950s America. Interestingly, the message of *The Day the Earth Stood Still* was so powerfully resonant in the Korean War era that it spurred an uncredited remake just three years later, Burt Balaban's *The Stranger from Venus* (1954), in which an alien (Helmut Dantine) comes to Earth to warn civilization of the imminent perils posed by nuclear weapons and falls in love with the sympathetic Susan North (Patricia Neal, essentially reprising her earlier role).

Fred M. Wilcox's *Forbidden Planet* (1956) offers an equally compact and convincing vision of the struggle between paradise and damnation in its tale of Dr. Edward Morbius (Walter Pidgeon), the reclusive master of Altair 4, an obscure planet on the edge of Earth's solar system. Commander John J. Adams (Leslie Nielsen) and his key staff members Lieutenant "Doc" Ostrow (Warren Stevens), Lieutenant Jerry Farman (Jack Kelly), and Chief Engineer Quinn (Richard Anderson) arrive on Altair 4 in an elegantly designed flying saucer ("United Planets Cruiser C-57-D") to investigate the disappearance of the earth spaceship *Bellerophon*, which vanished without a trace some twenty years earlier, leaving Dr. Morbius and his daughter Altaira (Anne Francis) as the only survivors on the planet, along with their companion Robby the robot (voiced by Marvin Miller), a device Morbius has cobbled together "in his spare time." When questioned by Commander Adams,

Morbius relates a seemingly fantastic story, claiming that nearly all the members of the *Bellerophon* party were killed in a single night by a mysterious force and that the surviving members of the expedition were vaporized along with their ship when they tried to escape. Only Morbius and Altaira have escaped this terrible fate, and in the ensuing twenty years, Morbius has built a paradise for himself and his daughter on Altair 4 and has no intentions of returning to Earth.

Adams is understandably skeptical of this story and becomes even more so when key elements of his spaceship's radio are smashed by an unknown intruder. Adams and "Doc" Ostrow return to Morbius's house to investigate, and eventually Morbius relates what he knows of the real circumstances on Altair 4: that it was once ruled by an omniscient and benevolent race called the Krel, who developed a series of "super computers" to control all the life-supporting functions on the planet. But, as with the members of the *Bellerophon* expedition, just as the Krel were on the verge of their greatest technological breakthrough, the use of computers to do away with all manual labor, the entire Krel race, too, perished in a single night without any rational explanation. Morbius conducts Adams and his key staff members on a tour of the Krel's staggeringly immense underground city and then tells them that, in view of what has transpired, the planet is "cursed" and Adams and his crew must leave immediately. Adams refuses and tells Morbius that "a find such as this must be placed under United Planetary control," a notion that Morbius immediately rejects; he is master of Altair 4 now.

In the film's harrowing conclusion, Adams, who has fallen in love with Altaira, is menaced along with his fellow crew members by a monstrous "creature from the Id," a synthetic creation "whistled up" from Morbius's unconscious mind as a concrete representation of his dislike for Adams's intrusion on Morbius's domain and Adams's love for his daughter, which threatens their extraterrestrial paradise. "Doc" Ostrow has divined Morbius's dark secret and confronts him with his responsibility for the deaths of the crew members of the *Bellerophon* and his resuscitation of the monster to do away with Adams and his crew.

27. Altaira (Anne Francis) at play in the synthetic Eden of Fred M. Wilcox's *Forbidden Planet* (1956). Photograph courtesy of The Jerry Ohlinger Archives.

Finally convinced that his artificially "amplified brain waves" (thanks to his appropriation of Krel technology) have brought about this disaster upon himself and his family, Morbius renounces the "creature from the Id" just as it is about to invade his futuristic house and destroy all its inhabitants. The outcome is now clear: the planet is cursed by the immense power of the Krel's huge chain of computers, which are able to materialize thought without regard for the eventual consequences. Instructed by Morbius, Adams triggers a detonation device that will destroy the entire planet in a short time, and Morbius begs Adams to take Altaira and depart. The couple leaves the planet in the nick of time, along with the surviving members of the crew. Far out in space, the crew of the C-57-D watches as Altair 4 explodes in a supernova of heat and light, sending shock waves far out into the universe.

The impact of *Forbidden Planet* in 1956 was immediate. It was MGM's first major foray into science fiction and was produced in Eastmancolor and CinemaScope at considerable expense. The special effects (the saucer landing, the monster from the Id) are deftly handled by animators from the Walt Disney studio, in concert with the superb set design of Arthur Lonergan, Hugh Hunt, and Edwin B. Willis. The music for the film represented another first: a completely electronic musical score composed by Louis and Bebe Barron using no conventional instrumentation whatsoever. The same feat would not be duplicated in a major Hollywood film until Bernard Herrmann's all-electronic score for Alfred Hitchcock's *The Birds* (1963). But most importantly, *Forbidden Planet* single-handedly elevated science fiction into a new and more respectable realm, as well as serving as the template for the work of an entire generation of younger filmmakers. What *Forbidden Planet* offers us most compellingly is a Miltonic vision of paradise lost. We have lived on Altair 4 and seen its wonders; now, they are no more. We can respool the film again and again, but our first glimpse of the Eden it offers will never be the same; we know now that it exists simply to be destroyed and that we must live as exiles beyond its vanished boundaries.

François Truffaut's only English-language film, *Fahrenheit 451* (1966), depicts a future society in which the "firemen" arrive to start fires rather than putting them out—fires that will consume libraries of books that are forbidden in the futuristic society in which the film is set. Such a scenario could hardly be called Edenic, and yet the outcome of the film depicts exactly that: a group of social dissidents, walking about in the snow, reciting books to each other in order to memorize them, determined to carry the written (or spoken) word forward. Sidney Pink's film *Journey to the Seventh Planet* (1962) is a curiously lavish low-budget science-fiction film featuring some excellent special-effects work by animator Jim Danforth. A group of astronauts land on Uranus and discover that their memories are being re-created for them by a giant brain beneath the surface of the planet. In a particularly memorable sequence, one of the astronauts reminisces about his childhood, describing a cottage where he spent his youth. The cottage and its surroundings magically appear behind him, silhouetted in the distance, gently backlit like a Maxfield Parrish lithograph. The film is marred by some unconvincing acting and poor dubbing but remains memorable to the present day. As with *Forbidden Planet,* emotions take on physical substance in *Journey to the Seventh Planet,* and once again, the only escape is to destroy the living central brain and flee the planet.

The power of the mind also plays a central role in Montgomery Tully's superb film *Escapement* (1957), a film that abrogates the function of sight through the use of a videotape "dream injection" machine. *Escapement*'s narrative is relatively straightforward, and yet Tully is most interested in the manner in which the machinery of legitimate scientific investigation may be used to "erase" the identity of an illusive authority figure who wishes to control the minds and thoughts (particularly the unconscious) of a select group of wealthy people. Dr. Phillip Maxwell (Meredith Edwards) has created a machine that is capable of "injecting" videotaped dream scenarios directly into the minds of his chosen subjects. Maxwell hopes to use his technique to soothe the troubled psyches of those who come to him seeking help

28. The illusion of love in Sidney Pink's *Journey to the Seventh Planet* (1962). Photograph courtesy of The Jerry Ohlinger Archives.

with drug addiction, chronic insomnia, alcoholism, and similar afflictions. However, Maxwell's financial backer, Paul Zakon (Peter Illing), decides to use Maxwell's invention to insinuate his own messianic personality into the mental landscape of Maxwell's clients.

In a bold departure from the film's seemingly conventional narrative style, we are allowed to view the images being imbedded in the minds of Zakon's victims. For the most part, the dream sequences, directed and choreographed by David Paltenghi, consist of mildly erotic heterotopic interludes, reminiscent of the 3-D sequences of Julian Roffman's *The Mask* (1961), or perhaps Salvador Dali's surrealist dream scenes in Alfred Hitchcock's *Spellbound* (1945). John Simmons's music for *Escapement* is, as in *Forbidden Planet*, entirely electronic, which adds considerably to the film's dreamlike detachment, particularly when coupled with Tully's carefully designed, trance-like camera work. The film also commands our attention in other ways, particularly in its examination of Zakon's abuses of the Edenic technology Maxwell has created.

Maxwell has created a series of synthetic environments that can help people escape drug addiction, personal trauma, and the general vicissitudes of existence, but Zakon has turned them to his own ends in a mad dream of world conquest. As interesting as the film is, the book on which it is based, by Charles Eric Maine, is even more ambitious. Maxwell's technology is hijacked by Zakon to create a worldwide network of "dream auditoriums" in which people lie in sleep tanks for months at a clip, drugged and fed through tubes, while their minds are filled with a series of endless Utopic images that make a return to

29. Paul Zakon (Peter Illing), left, and his assistants manufacture synthetic dreams for mass consumption in Montgomery Tully's *Escapement* (1957). Photograph courtesy of The Jerry Ohlinger Archives.

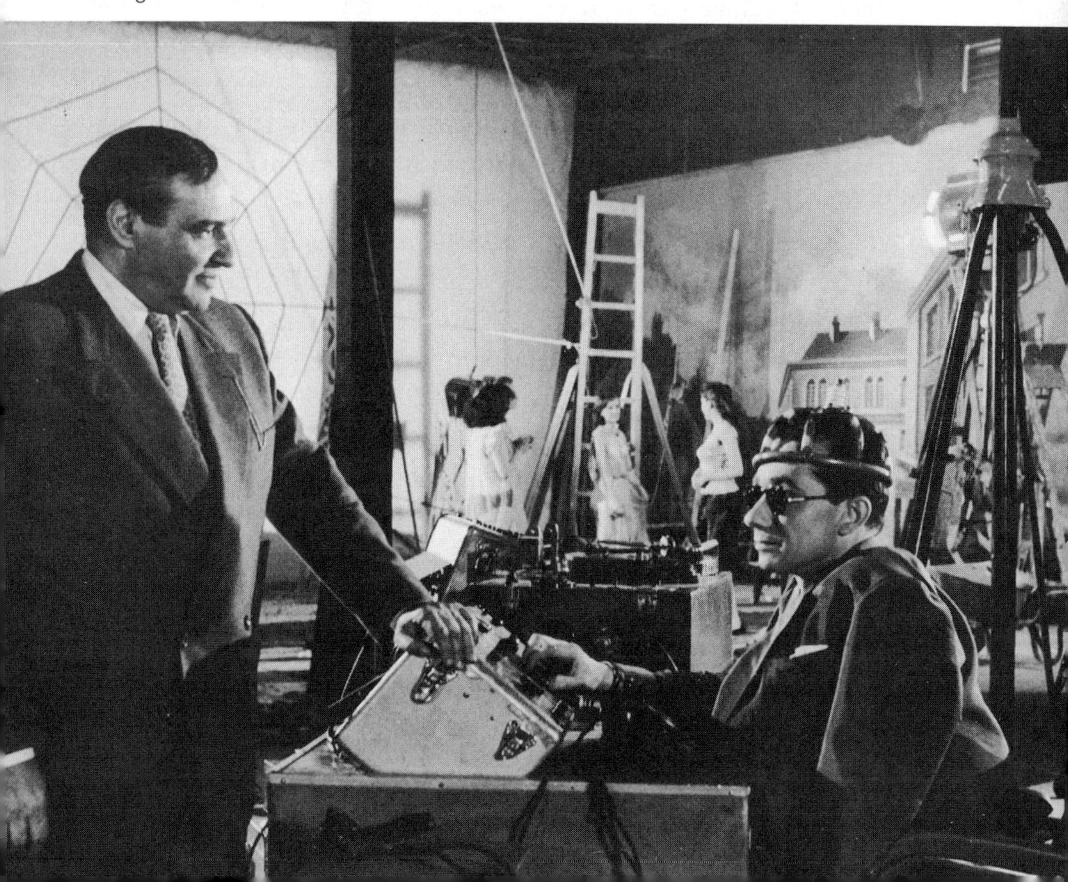

real life almost unbearable. Zakon's empire expands until millions of people are stuck in a semipermanent deep freeze of dreams, allowing Zakon to take control of their real lives on the outside and strip them of their money and possessions. At length Maxwell manages to break free of Zakon's influence and elects a drastic remedy: he murders Zakon with a hammer and "records" the murder on a dream tape, which he then forces Zakon's technicians to feed into the brains of his millions of semiconscious subjects. Maxwell wishes only to rouse these paradise-addicted slumberers from their Utopic torpor but discovers that the tape of Zakon's murder is so intense that his recorded death becomes the actual death of all his somnolent clients. The spell is broken, and the dream chambers are abolished, but Maxwell, as the book ends, is being tried for 12 million "psychic murders"—an outcome he never imagined possible.

As an echo of this more apocalyptic scenario, an interesting subplot in the film's narrative revolves around the introduction of a singularly minor character, Signore Pietro Kallini (Carol Borelli), who comes to the dream clinic seeking relief from addiction to heroin. The film unflinchingly depicts the consequences of Kallini's addiction: his arms are punctuated with a large number of needle marks, which are shown in a graphic close-up (a rather surprising image for a 1950s film). Significantly, we never learn precisely what happens to Kallini. He is outfitted with an electronic skullcap to facilitate the "injection" of the dream images, then trundled off to a morgue-like holding area in which all of the patients are required to lie on a series of beds that roll into the wall. This is the last we see of him. Tully is also fascinated with the mechanics of the "dream injection process." The clinic functions as a taping studio, where throughout the film we see dancers and other performers rehearsing the sequences that will be electronically transmitted into the brains of the clinic's patients.

Thus in *Escapement*, what we see is immaterial. All visual stimuli are recorded directly on videotape, using the filter of the video lens as a transmission field, and then relayed directly into the brain of the subject through digital electronic impulses. *Escapement*'s vision of paradise, though electronically induced, is nevertheless a complete, coherent, and compelling universe. Although Dr. Zakon uses his device to illicit ends, its inventor, Dr. Maxwell, created the device to allow the human mind to artificially experience paradise. The machinery of Heaven has thus been put to the wrong use, but this is not the fault of its inventor; it is what happens when commerce and greed intersect with the Edenic impulse.

This is what the most positive and enriching science-fiction attempts to do; to offer a positive spin on contemporary culture and extrapolate the best of all possible outcomes as the realm of the future. Disaster has its charms, but regeneration, as in Douglas Trumbull's *Silent Running* (1971), offers us a sense of hope that the prehistoric behemoth in Eugène Lourié's *The Beast from 20,000 Fathoms* (1953), the dystopian predations of the giant ants in Gordon Douglas's *Them!* (1954), the bug-eyed invaders in Edward L. Cahn's *Invasion of the Saucer Men* (1957), or the gigantic sea serpent in Sidney Pink's *Reptilicus* (1962) will never deliver. The only way to effectively deal with the Venusian Ymir, a reptilian creature that grows larger with passing hours, is to kill him, as the military finally does in Nathan Juran's *20 Million Miles to Earth* (1957). Although he has been resurrected countless times, when we go to see films in the Godzilla series, we seek epic displays of destruction (the loss of life and property) together with the concomitant death(s) of the monsters (Godzilla, Mothra, Ghidra, Rodan, and their kin) who initiated the cycle of violence in the first place. The only victory in dystopian science-fiction is death; the only rationale for death is more death, and more destruction. Thus the cycle is locked, and allows us no surcease from endless repetition.

So if, in the famous phrase used at the end of the 1951 version of *The Thing*, we are to "keep watching the skies," we should perhaps seek portents of our future world, rather than talismans of our imminent destruction. We have opened the door; what transpires now should be an act of faith, rather than the embrace of disaster. No one can deny that we live in an era of great uncertainty, in which cataclysmic changes are potentially possible and new wars seem to be erupting around the globe with each new day. Yet, for every story that revels in details of death and destruction, there is an alternative tale to tell, though perhaps it is not as well publicized. For every tale of disaster, there is an opposing vision of life being renewed.

In addition to the films discussed in this volume, from *Journey to the Seventh Planet* to *Valerie and Her Week of Wonders*, from the *Beach Party* films to *Elvira Madigan*, there are thousands of additional Edenic and Utopian films hidden in the shadows of cinema history. Peter Whitehead's nearly forgotten and all but unavailable *Tonite Let's All Make Love in London* (1967) is a paean to the counterculture that embraces the essence of 1960s hedonism; René Clair's *Liberty for Us* (*À nous la liberté*, 1931) is a gentle satire in which machines do the work of men, not so that they can be displaced from their jobs but rather so that they can picnic, fish, bowl, play cards, and make love in a meadow. Jean Renoir's unfinished *A Day in the Country* (*Une partie de campagne*, shot in 1936, released in 1946, and finally released on DVD in 2003 with forty-two minutes of previously unseen outtakes, in what might be regarded as the definitive "incomplete" version) exists in a world of summer splendor, where romantic dalliances and leisurely ways of life dominate the marginal narrative proceedings. Indeed, there is little more to the film than what its title suggests—"A Day in the Country"—and yet within the film's modest compass, all of human life is on display.

The brilliant filmmaker Jean-Luc Godard, still directing films after nearly half a century, interrogates many of the questions explored in this volume in his *Our Music* (*Notre Musique*, 2004), a detailed outline of the mechanics of Hell, Purgatory, and Heaven, and the manner in which man makes his own Heaven or Hell as a direct result of his actions on earth. The film is typically Godardian in its avoidance of traditional narrative, with eccentric shot design and elliptical editing. But the film is also unusually "optimistic" for Godard, whose dystopian science-fiction masterpiece *Alphaville* (1965), a typically cynical work from the director, depicts a future world in which humans have become robots, slaves to a technological dictatorship, controlled by the passionless electronic "conscience" of a giant computer, Alpha 60.

Our Music, in contrast, is a passionate defense of the human spirit in the face of war. In *Our Music*, Hell is a ten-minute montage of unbelievable density, in which video-manipulated images of war, violence, and destruction culled from Hollywood films, newsreels, and captured battleground footage play out with inexorable brutality against the backdrop of a sparse, angular sound track. The middle section, Purgatory, takes place at a intellectual conference held in the city of Sarajevo, scarred by the recent events of battle, in which Godard and a group of similarly inclined colleagues discuss the various representations of war in the cinema, and Godard, in particular, addresses the inherent unreliability of film grammar in depicting relationships between men and women. Subsequently, snipers kill a young woman who has attended the conference when they mistake her for a terrorist; apparently, in the eyes of the soldiers, her red schoolbag full of books has marked her as a suicide bomber. The film's final section takes place in Heaven, which is guarded by a group of marines, as the young woman luxuriates in her new surroundings, a verdant forest where people relax, play, make love, and generally pursue the pastime of being truly human; that is, existing in an absence of conflict, in harmony with the design of nature. In a discussion of *Our Music* with critic Manohla Dargis, Godard noted that the process of making a film involves a certain kind of circularity, in which the production process becomes the film itself through repetition. As the filmmaker explained, "in the movies you have one image, then another, then another and then another and finally there's a past, present and future. It's a metaphor for some profound things in the history of humanity. You have production, economically and sociologically, then you have distribution, and then there is exploitation, this terrible word" (qtd. in Dargis 22).

In essence Godard is saying that "all filmed images are filmed reality" (22), inviting us to partake of the world in its genuine essence, without the mediation of technology, if we can appreciate them in their most originary sense—that is, in the closest relation to life itself. As Godard notes in the interview, "to live is to survive," and by embracing the living, we can celebrate the reality of our corporeal

30. Jean-Luc Godard in the late 1980s, in his studio. Photograph courtesy of The Jerry Ohlinger Archives.

existence, our hold on the world of the living, both within the cinema and in the world that informs the construction of its disparate images—the domain of life itself (22). As a voiceover in *Our Music* tells us directly, the purpose of cinema is to "guide us through the night and bring us to the light," which is precisely the work that the film accomplishes.

For Heaven is indeed on Earth. Robert Rossen's last film, *Lilith* (1964), exists in a sensuous world of light and shadow, telling the tale of young psychiatric intern Vincent Bruce (Warren Beatty), who gradually falls under the spell of the title character, played by Jean Seberg. By the film's end, Beatty's character is loath to leave the safety of the hospital grounds where Lilith and her troubled friends are confined;

the prison has become a zone of safety, a place of respite and peace. The problems of the real world seem remote and unthreatening; in his own way, Vincent Bruce has found a Heaven where responsibility can be freely abandoned. Frank Launder's *The Belles of St. Trinian's* (1954) takes place in a similar institutional setting; this time it is a renegade boarding school for "problem" girls, presided over by Miss Millicent Fritton, the matronly headmistress of the failing establishment (played by Alastair Sim in very convincing drag). The schoolgirls at St. Trinian's are unreformed degenerates by any measurable social standard; they use the school chemistry lab to distill bootleg gin, steal horses to fix the outcome of sporting events, and treat soccer games with rival schools as all-out warfare with the highest possible body count of the members of the opposing team the ultimate goal.

When officials from the Ministry of Education are dispatched to the school to restore order, they are seduced by the older students into staying as permanent guests in a lotus land of alcoholic decadence. The teachers are never paid, and when the daughter of a rich Middle Eastern potentate arrives with a large sum of money for her personal allowance, Miss Fritton immediately confiscates (and spends) her money "as a precautionary measure." And yet, as you might have guessed, the entire film is a comedy, a broad satire on the British public school system, and all of the film's participants delight in carrying the resultant burlesque to its absolute limits. Time has no real meaning at St. Trinian's, and there is no real end of term—there will always be a new crop of acolytes ready to be initiated into the rites of the academy and the delights of heedless indolence.

Other examples of the Edenic cinema proliferate, encompassing both the worlds of security and moral complacency found in cinematic small-town life as well as the realms of cosmopolitan sexual playfulness. Carefree socialites cavort through a lost Parisian landscape of pleasure and romantic dalliance in Lewis Milestone's *Paris in Spring* (1935); James Cagney takes a break from his numerous gangster roles to play an itinerant newspaperman in a sleepy small town in William K. Howard's *Johnny Come Lately* (1943); Elvis Presley croons his way through the minimal complications of Norman Taurog's idyllic *Blue Hawaii* (1961). Alain Berliner's *My Life in Pink* (*Ma vie en rose*, 1997) tells the story of Ludovic (then seven-year-old Georges Du Fresne), a young boy who refuses to accept his assigned gender role and persists in dressing up as a young girl, hoping to marry the boy next door, much to the consternation of his parents. To escape from reality, he and his grandmother watch a children's television show, *The World of Pam*, in which a fantasyland figure of feminine domesticity sets the rules for young French girls to follow to meet the ideal man. Ludovic completely immerses himself in Pam's world to the point that even his indulgent grandmother becomes alarmed; at work, his father is ostracized because his son is "a queer." Ludovic knows nothing of what society expects of him; all he knows is what he wants, and that Pam is his ideal role model. Events veer toward tragedy but then resolve themselves as Ludovic realizes that he cannot carry his childhood fantasy forward into adulthood—much to the relief of his beleaguered parents. Similarly, another world is created in Philippe de Broca's *That Man from Rio* (*L'homme de Rio*, 1964), where Jean-Paul Belmondo drifts through a phantasmal Rio de Janeiro in search of a lost diamond, surrounded by thieves and assassins at every step, but none of it is taken seriously; the nominal scenario is really an excuse for some clever acrobatics and extended sequences of spirited calypso dancing, filmed in riotous color.

Andy Warhol's films were noted for their structured decadence in his early sound period (roughly 1964–on), but he began his career with such Edenic silent films as *Kiss* (1963–1964), described as "a lip-smacking revue with numbers and routines showing the many styles of the kiss" (FMC 151); the six-and-a-half-hour *Sleep* (1963–1964), in which poet John Giorno dozes soundly as Warhol's camera gazes upon his supine body with somnolent reverence; *Empire* (1964), an eight-hour "homage to the world's tallest building"; as well as the equally contemplative *Haircut* (1963), *Eat* (1963), and *Blow Job* (1963), in which, famously, only the head of a young man is seen while offscreen an oral sex act is performed on him to his obvious delight. In these simple,

31. Andy Warhol and Ivan Karp in Warhol's studio in the early 1960s. Photograph courtesy of The Jerry Ohlinger Archives.

static films, Warhol was not only teaching himself how to make movies; he was also reinventing the cinema, as George Méliès, Alice Guy Blaché, the Lumière brothers, and other pioneers of the cinema had done three-quarters of a century before. As with Brakhage, Warhol was "re-seeing" the cinematic image for the first time, with a child's vision, concentrating on the supposedly mundane and the obvious to create a renewed universe in which even the simplest acts are worthy of sustained contemplation.

The world is forever new, forever waiting to be reinvented, and re-seen, by each new generation. What stops our progress toward Eden is a stasis of imagery; we can't imagine seeing something in a new way simply because we're so used to seeing it in a fashion embraced by the dominant media. Warhol's concentration on the simplest of acts—sleeping, getting a haircut, eating—brought cinema back full circle to the days of the Edison kinetoscopes such as *Fred Ott's Sneeze* (1894) and *The Kiss* (1896)—showing sneezing and kissing—and other early experiments with the moving image. Warhol's way of viewing the world was revolutionary because he dared to see everything as being new again, as being equally worthy of celebration as well as our interest and attention. One could argue that the serial repetition of the tightly framed images in Warhol's work are Edenic overkill, but as Warhol himself argued, "it's a way of expressing oneself. All my images are the same . . . but very different at the same time. . . . They change with the light of colors, with the times and the moods. . . . Isn't life a series of images that change as they repeat themselves?" (qtd. in Dillenberger 116). Paradise is a state of grace, a state of being in which everything is new and ceaselessly renewable, simply because we have taken the time to carefully observe the world around us. The wonder of being simply is; it is the raw material of the future, the essence of our dreams and hopes. The cinema, at its most Edenic, can restore us to a state of natural wonder in which we are encouraged to contemplate the visual and tactile world as virgin terrain.

In all of the films discussed in this volume, then, "utopia is art. It has an expressive as well as a communicative function" (Morrison 140), which is why it is so well suited to the medium of the cinema. As Seiji Nuita argues, "Utopia can be used as a barometer to measure the life-energy of a nation; if a race or a people lives vigorously in world history, it will produce utopias befitting its vigor" (32). Adds Joseph Gusfield, "the present, as it exists today in the world, is also a future for others in the same world" (81). Indeed, "hope is generated at the interface between the past and the future" (Rycroft 7) and constitutes "an active waiting for a future that is open . . . and helps to prepare the future in some way by its very expectation of it" (Nowotny 57).

In short, the future lies before us, waiting to be invented; what we do with this implicit promise is both our most crucial responsibility and our greatest opportunity for change. Because of this, "hoping is really only a concession that we have reached the limits of our agency. Unable to secure what we desire, we place our confidence in, and so give ourselves over to, the caprice of forces beyond our control" (Shade 4). This is the only way that true progress can be made, by giving ourselves over to the power of reinvention, of ceaseless becoming. At the same time, we must guard against the "danger in the media's embrace of fear and worry [because] we waste precious energy and also poison our horizons of meaning in doing so" (Shade 203). And yet, "the sharing of dreams can lead to heightened creativity, improved mental health, and even a more peaceful and cooperative culture. Moreover, the dreams themselves can be shaped or controlled to bring about these benefits" (Domhoff 5).

32. Three frames from Andy Warhol's *Empire* (1964). Photograph courtesy of The Jerry Ohlinger Archives.

The cinema is our repository of dreams, of visions of the world we wish to inhabit, of the lives we might hope to live. At the same time, it also gestures toward the future while incorporating the visions and lessons of the past. What is cinema if not the record of human progress and failure over the past one hundred years? From the earliest documentary films of the Lumière brothers and the exotic trick films of Georges Méliès, the cinema has offered us a tactile, palpably real zone that we continually seek to inhabit and emulate, a series of instructions, if you will, on how to live one's life. The films discussed in this volume offer us moments out of time, moments in which the human condition is bearable, in which our hopes and dreams can become concrete, and the cares of everyday existence momentarily cease to be of any consequence. Eden in the cinema is a real place, a space that has been cleared for us by the practitioners of the moving image to form an oasis in the tumult of modern culture, a time out of time in which we can contemplate our past and future. It is one of the sacred spaces of modern society.

What does the cinema constitute, if not an amorphous, ever-expanding dream of the human condition in both its most positive and most negative aspects? In the 1960s, when the dominant cinema first began to break down through the agency of small film societies and university film groups, 16mm film was the medium of choice to spread the history of cinema, existing outside the artificial realms of canon, to new and highly receptive audiences. Now, in the twenty-first century, this renegade practice of "chamber screenings" is being continued in the digital age with clandestine screenings of non-mainstream films for an even newer audience, for whom our shared cinematic past is often a world of mystery, quickly receding into the pages of history texts that become the films themselves when the films lose their actual availability to general audiences. These guerrilla screenings, conducted much like "raves," take place in parking lots, abandoned warehouses, and open fields—anywhere an image can be projected. As Chris Thompson reports,

> For three years, cult-movie buffs have been organizing "guerrilla drive-ins" in a number of cities, rigging together a nest of digital

> projectors, DVD players, and radio transmitters or stereo speakers, spreading the word online, and assembling on parking lots or fields to watch obscure films beneath the stars. They project the image onto warehouses or bridge pillars, tune their car stereos to a designated FM frequency, and sit back and enjoy the show. The only thing they do not do is ask for permission. [As Wes Modes, one of the new breed of digital guerrillas, noted], "Part of why we're doing this is to reclaim public space and give people a way to use the nighttime that's not mediated by commerce," he said. "In our town, the parks close at sundown, you have to buy something at coffee shops. We wanted to give people a way to interact with each other outdoors without having to spend any money." (E1, E4)

In this way, these admittedly illicit screenings bring the films of the past to the present without the cumbersome detritus of 16mm reels, splicers, and film itself; the entire experience is digitized. Perhaps the quality isn't as good as with first-run 35mm projection, but that's not the point. Without Wes Modes and his colleagues, most of the films screened at these impromptu sessions would never reach an audience at all. It's this, or nothing. Clearly, this mode of presentation is the only truly egalitarian solution.

The cinema is constantly dying and constantly being reborn, renewing itself in the visions of those who make, preserve, and project the films of the past and present. One of the most attractive aspects of these guerrilla screenings is that they have done away with the institution of the movie theater itself; anywhere there is a digital projector and an audience, a screening can commence. There are no tickets, no audience regulations beyond those of mutual respect among the audience members, and as Modes notes, these screenings are thus "not mediated by commerce." Rather, they are inspired by a vision of equal access to any images that one can burn off a DVD, a world in which all artificial barriers and gatekeepers collapse, their phantom authority exhausted.

This book started with a look at John Pierson's trip to Fiji in search of a lost paradise, a paradise that existed not only in the physical presence of the tropics but also on the cinema screen of the 180 Meridian Cinema, where he ran free films for the island's populace despite some local opposition from the religious authorities. Pierson's desire was for a dual escape, not only from the rigors and competitive struggle of life in Manhattan but also for an escape into the movies themselves, stripped of their commercial trappings, exhibited as unique exemplars, without all the attendant publicity that is part of the dominant Hollywood cinema. This book ends with that same dream, albeit accomplished on a more modest scale: screenings of films for the public, who can attend these clandestine projections without payment, enjoying a social moment in the presence of the cinema without having to engage in the vicissitudes of commerce.

This very notion of getting something for free, devoid of commerciality, is at the heart of both enterprises and represents the purest Eden instinct of the cinema. When I was in my teens in New Brunswick, New Jersey, we used to have all-night screenings of cartoons, newsreels, serials, and experimental films projected on a sheet tied between two trees in people's backyards, while the audience—men, women, and children—took in the spectacle from the comfort of their blankets on the grass, eating dinner, drinking wine, involved in the simultaneous spectacle of the actual and the imaginary. And similar screenings took place elsewhere, on the road in San Francisco, London, Paris, in backyards in Brooklyn. One of the communal aspects of the 1960s was that everyone in the filmmaking community had a 16mm projector, and "chamber screenings" were common, with people arriving for dinner with something to contribute to the meal and a reel of film in their arms. The film dominated the twilight landscape, but at the same time, children would run behind the screen to catch the action from the other side; couples would dreamily contemplate their future while watching visions of the past; and older viewers would contentedly dream of the past as they remembered the images on the screen in front of them as memories from their youth. It was a shared feast of images, one of the most Edenic aspects of those times; cinema without walls.

The collapse of the 16mm market changed all that—I remember when it was possible to rent a feature film for as little as $6 plus shipping, and a cartoon or Three Stooges short for a few dollars more—and home video has created a new, more insular experience, in which the embrace of community is denied. Sitting alone in our houses, watching our giant-screen televisions, we participate in a phantom community, not a real one, for all the supposed "interactivity" at our command. The days of all-night festivals, such as the ones that used to occupy the screen at the National Film Theater in London, are long gone, replaced by memories in a DVD box to be shared with only a few members of the family or with friends. Both Pierson and the new video renegades share one common dream: the idea of free movies for the public at large, as a part of the spectacle but not the entire experience. By bringing the public back to the movies, by making films accessible to all, the new breed of roving, subterranean video projectionists are returning the images of our collective past to the populace at large, to be enjoyed by the audience as members of a bonded community. When theatrical distribution peaked in 1946, television had yet to become a commonplace reality. Now, with everyone neatly tucked in their own house, yet cut off from their neighbors, it is time to return the cinema to the public sphere, and in so doing, capture some measure of its innocence and egalitarian spirit.

The visions of paradise discussed in this volume, then, most properly belong here, in the eyes and minds of those who can actualize them. In the new world, access to cinema will be open to all, and as the films examined in this text testify, that world is real and tangible, if we will only open our eyes and hearts to it.

WORKS CITED

American Experience. "Presidential Politics: Franklin D. Roosevelt, 32nd President." November 16, 2004 ‹www.pbs.org/wgbh/amex/presidents/32_f_roosevelt/f_roosevelt_politics.html›.

Andrews, Suzanna. "Hostage to Fortune." *Vanity Fair* December 2004: 292–303.

Belhmer, Rudy, ed. *W. S. Van Dyke's Journal: White Shadows in the South Seas (1927–1928).* Lanham, MD: Scarecrow, 1996.

Bernstein, Matthew. *Walter Wanger: Hollywood Independent.* Minneapolis: University of Minnesota Press, 1994.

Biner, Pierre. *The Living Theater.* Trans. Robert Meister. New York: Avon Books, 1972.

Bogdanovich, Peter. *Fritz Lang in America.* New York: Praeger, 1967.

Borte, Jason. "Bud Browne." *Surfline.* October 2000. 10 November 2004 ‹http://www.surfline.com/surfaz/browne_bud.cfm›.

———. "José Angel," *Surfline.* October 2000. 10 November 2004 ‹http://www.surfline.com/surfaz/angel_jose.cfm›.

Brown, Bruce. "Slippery When Wet." *Wetsand.com.* 12 November 2004 ‹http://www.wetsand.com/store/product.asp?Prodid=1180›.

Cripps, Thomas. *Slow Fade to Black: The Negro in American Film 1900–1942.* London: Oxford University Press, 1977.

———. *Black Film as Genre.* Bloomington: Indiana University Press, 1979.

Dargis, Manohla. "Godard's Metaphysics of the Movies." *New York Times* 21 November 2004, sec. 2: 22.

De Apple Press Release. "On Patrol in De Appel," notes for video installation show. De Appel Gallery, Amsterdam, Holland, January 29–March 20, 2005.

Deming, Mark. "The Blood of Jesus." 16 November 2004 ‹http://www.allmovie.com/cg/avg.dll›.

Dillenberger, Jane Daggett. *The Religious Art of Andy Warhol.* New York: Continuum, 1998.

Dixon, Wheeler Winston. "When I'm 63: An Interview with Jonathan Miller." *Popular Culture Review* 10.1 (February 1999): 1–11.

———. "Performativity in 1960s American Experimental Cinema: The Body as Site of Ritual and Display." *Film Criticism* 23.1 (Fall 1998): 48–60.

Domhoff, G. William. *The Mystique of Dreams: A Search for Utopia Through the Senoi Dream Factory*. Berkeley: University of California Press, 1985.

Ehrenstein, David. "Saint Warren." *Film Culture* 46 (Autumn 1967): 19.

Eliel, Carol S. "Interpreting Tradition: Mariko Mori's *Nirvana*." *Mariko Mori*. Ed. Kevin E. Consey and Julia Peyton-Jones. Chicago: Museum of Contemporary Art, 1998. 27–32.

Film-Makers' Cooperative Catalogue No. 4, The. New York: New American Cinema Group, 1967.

Ganguly, Suranjan. "Stan Brakhage: The 60th Birthday Interview." *Experimental Cinema: The Film Reader*. Ed. Wheeler Winston Dixon and Gwendolyn Audrey Foster. New York: Routledge, 2002. 139–162.

Gusfield, Joseph. "Economic Development as a Modern Utopia." *Aware of Utopia*. Ed. David W. Plath. Urbana: University of Illinois Press, 1971. 75–85.

Heyman, J. D. "The Piersons: A Movie Honcho Moves His Family to Fiji." *People* 3 February 2003. 19 September 2003 ‹http://www.grainypictures.com/people.html›.

Higgie, Jennifer. "Get It While You Can: Jennifer Higgie on Janice Kerbel." *Frieze.com*. 2 March 2005 ‹http://www.frieze.com/feature_single.asp?f=929›.

Hoberman, Jim. *On Jack Smith's "Flaming Creatures" and Other Secret-Flix of Cinemaroc*. New York: Granary Books, 2001.

Hudson, Alexandra. "East Germany Becoming a Retro Utopia 15 Years On." *Reuters News Online*. 9 November 2004. 10 November 2004 ‹http://www.reuters.com/newsArticle.jhtml?type=ourWorldNews&storyID=6758116›.

Hughes, Robert. *Heaven and Hell in Western Art*. New York: Stein and Day, 1968.

Inoguchi, Rikihei, and Tadashi Nakajima, with Roger Pineau. *The Divine Wind: Japan's Kamikaze Force in World War II*. Rpt. 1958. Annapolis: Naval Institute Press, 1994.

James, David E. *Allegories of Cinema: American Film in the Sixties*. Princeton: Princeton University Press, 1989.

Jenkins, Henry. "Exploiting Feminism in Stephanie Rothman's *Terminal Island* (1973)." 3 March 2005 ‹http://web.mit.edu/21fms/www/faculty/henry3/publications.html›.

"John Pierson Interview." *Crave Online*. 13 February 2005 ‹http://www.craveonline.com/filmtv/stories.php?sid=1083›.

Jones, G. William. *Black Cinema Treasures: Lost and Found*. Denton, TX: University of North Texas Press, 1991.

Kampion, Drew. "Bruce Brown." *Surfline.* October 2000. 11 November 2004 ‹http://www.surfline.com/surfaz/brown_bruce.cfm›.

———."Endless Summer." *Surfline.* May 2000. 11 November 2004 ‹http://www.surfline.com/surfaz/endless_summer.cfm›.

———. "John Severson," *Surfline.* October 2000. 12 November 2004 ‹http://www.surfline.com/surfaz/severson_john.cfm›.

Kehr, Dave. "Fiji Favorites: Guys in Dresses." *New York Times* 5 September 2003, B6.

Kerouac, Jack. "Essentials of Spontaneous Prose." *Evergreen Review* 2.5 (Summer 1958): 72–73.

Kinnard, Roy and Tim Davis. *Divine Images: A History of Jesus on the Screen.* New York: Citadel, 1992.

Kitses, Jim. *Horizons West: Directing the Western from John Ford to Clint Eastwood.* Bloomington: Indiana University Press, 1970.

Klocker, Hubert. "Gesture and the Object: Liberation as Aktion: A European Component of Performative Art." *Out of Actions: Between Performance and the Object, 1949–1979.* Ed. Paul Schimmel. Los Angeles: Museum of Contemporary Art/Thames and Hudson, 1998. 159–195.

Krzywinska, Tanya. "*Valerie and Her Week of Wonders.*" *Kinoeye.* 11 November 2004 ‹http://www.kinoeye.org/03/09/krzywinska09.php›.

Landler, Mark. "Slaves for Vacation: Europe Ponders the Meaning of Life." *New York Times* 15 August 2004, sec 4: 1, 3.

Maine, Charles Eric. *Escapement.* London: Hodder & Stoughton, 1956.

Martin, Jean-Clet. "Of Images and Worlds: Toward a Geology of the Cinema." *The Brain Is the Screen: Deleuze and the Philosophy of Cinema.* Ed. Gregory Flaxman. Minneapolis: University of Minnesota Press, 2000. 61–85.

McMahan, Alison. *Alice Guy Blaché: Lost Visionary of the Cinema.* New York: Continuum, 2002.

Mekas, Jonas. *Movie Journal: The Rise of a New American Cinema 1959–1971.* New York: Macmillan, 1972.

Miller, Donald L. and Henry Steele Commager. *The Story of World War II.* New York: Simon & Schuster, 2001.

Morris, Gary. "Beyond the Beach: AIP's Beach Party Movies." *Bright Lights Film Journal* 11 November 2004 ‹http://www.brightlightsfilm.com/21/21_beach.html›.

Morrison, Alasdair. "Uses of Utopia." *Utopias.* Ed. Peter Alexander and Roger Gill. LaSalle, IL: Open Court, 1984. 139–151.

Nowotny, Joan. "Despair and the Object of Hope." *The Sources of Hope.* Ed. Ross Fitzgerald. Oxford: Pergamon, 1979. 44–66.

Nuita, Seiji. "Traditional Utopias in Japan and the West: A Study in Contrasts."

Aware of Utopia. Ed. David W. Plath. Urbana: University of Illinois Press, 1971. 12–32.

Ottoson, Robert L. *American International Pictures: A Filmography*. New York: Garland, 1985.

Parish, James Robert. *Ghosts and Angels in Hollywood Films*. Jefferson, NC: McFarland, 1994.

Pierson, Georgia. "Fiji Essay." January 2003. 19 September 2003 ‹http://www.grainypictures.com/fiji/georgiafiji.html›.

Pierson, Janet. "General Fiji Report—March [2003]." 19 September 2003 ‹http://www.grainypictures.com/fiji/march.html›.

Pierson, John. "Facts & Fibs." *People* 3 February 2003. 19 September 2003 ‹http://www.grainypictures.com/people.html›.

———. "Isle of Forgotten Fans." *Los Angeles Times* 21 July 2002. 19 September 2003 ‹http://www.grainypictures.com/latimesfiji.html›.

———. "Showing Free Movies in Fiji: Is He an Ugly American?" *Los Angeles Times* 8 December 2002. 19 September 2003 ‹http://www.grainypictures.com/latimesfiji1.html›.

Principality of New Utopia. 20 February 2005 ‹http://www.carbonfusion.com/utopia/›.

Renan, Sheldon. *An Introduction to the American Underground Film*. New York: Dutton, 1967.

Rice, Ron. "Foundation for the Invention and Creation of Absurd Movies." *Film Culture* 39 (Winter 1965): 117.

Rist, Pipilloti. *Katalog: Kunsthalle Zürich, Musée d'Art Modern de la Ville de Paris*. Paris: Editions de la Ville de Paris, 1999. Unpaginated.

———. Promotional flyer for Pipilloti Rist exhibit at the Luhring Augustine Gallery, New York City. 11 September 2004.

Rosenbaum, Jonathan. "*Tabu*." *Chicago Reader*. 16 January 2005 ‹http://spacefinder.chicagoreader.com/movies/capsules/08009_TABU.html›.

Roud, Richard. *Jean-Marie Straub*. New York: Viking, 1972.

Rycroft, Charles. "Steps to an Ecology of Hope." *The Sources of Hope*. Ed. Ross Fitzgerald. Oxford: Pergamon, 1979. 3–23.

Sargeant, Jack. *Naked Lens: Beat Cinema*. London: Creation Books, 1997.

Scheib, Richard. "*Heaven Can Wait*." 1990. 16 November 2004 ‹http://www.moria.co.nz/fantasy/heavencanwait43.htm›.

Schimmel, Paul. "Leap into the Void: Performance and the Object." *Out of Actions: Between Performance and the Object, 1949–1979*. Ed. Paul Schimmel. Los Angeles: Museum of Contemporary Art/Thames and Hudson, 1998. 17–119.

Shade, Patrick. *Habits of Hope: A Pragmatic Theory*. Nashville: Vanderbilt University Press, 2000.

Sonbert, Warren. Unpublished interview with Wheeler Winston Dixon. New York, 15 May 1969.

Staehling, Richard. "From *Rock Around the Clock* to *The Trip*: The Truth About Teen Movies." *Kings of the Bs: Working within the Hollywood System.* Ed. Todd McCarthy and Charles Flynn. New York: Dutton, 1975. 220–251.

"Stan Brakhage Biography." 23 February 2005 ‹http://www.imdb.com/name/nm0104132/bio›.

Stiles, Kristine. "Uncorrupted Joy: International Art Actions." *Out of Actions: Between Performance and the Object, 1949–1979.* Ed. Paul Schimmel. Los Angeles: Museum of Contemporary Art/Thames and Hudson, 1998. 227–329.

Strawn, Linda May. "Interview with Samuel Z. Arkoff." *Kings of the Bs: Working within the Hollywood System.* Ed. Todd McCarthy and Charles Flynn. New York: Dutton, 1975. 255–268.

"Surfing History." *Hemispheres* November 2004, 117.

Thompson, Chris. "Now Playing, A Digital Brigadoon." *New York Times* 29 July 2004, E1, E4.

Wells, H. G. "The Honour and Dignity of the Free Mind." *Travels of a Republican Radical in Search of Hot Water.* Middlesex: Penguin, 1939. 122–150.

Wykes, Alan. *H. G. Wells in the Cinema.* London: Jupiter, 1977.

INDEX

Note: Page numbers in bold denote illustrations.

ABOUT THE AUTHOR

Wheeler Winston Dixon is the James Ryan Endowed Professor of Film Studies, Professor of English at the University of Nebraska, Lincoln, and, with Gwendolyn Audrey Foster, editor-in-chief of the *Quarterly Review of Film and Video.* His newest books as author or editor include *American Cinema of the 1940s: Themes and Variations* (Rutgers University Press, 2005); *Lost in the Fifties: Recovering Phantom Hollywood* (Southern Illinois University Press, 2005); *Film and Television after 9/11* (editor; Southern Illinois University Press, 2004); *Visions of the Apocalypse: Spectacles of Destruction in American Cinema* (Wallflower, 2003); *Straight: Constructions of Heterosexuality in the Cinema* (State University of New York Press, 2003), and *Experimental Cinema: The Film Reader,* co-edited with Gwendolyn Audrey Foster (Routledge, 2002). On April 11–12, 2003, he was honored with a retrospective of his films at the Museum of Modern Art in New York, and his films were acquired for the permanent collection of the museum.